A SHEPHERD'S DELIGHT

A James Hogg Anthology

A
SHEPHERD'S
DELIGHT

A James Hogg Anthology

edited by Judy Steel

CANONGATE
1985

First published in 1985
by Canongate Publishing Limited
17 Jeffrey Street, Edinburgh

British Library Cataloguing in Publication Data
Hogg, James, *1770-1835*
A shepherd's delight: a James Hogg anthology
I. Title   II. Steel, Judy
828'.709   PR4791

ISBN 0-86241-106-8
ISBN 0-86241-088-6 Pbk

The publishers acknowledge the financial assistance
of the Scottish Arts Council
in the publication of this volume.

Typeset by Studioscope/Mainstream Publishing, Edinburgh
Printed and bound by Clark Constable, Edinburgh

for my family

CONTENTS

Introduction 1

Acknowledgements 17

Life in the Valleys
    A Boy's Song 20
    The Poachers 22
    Gemel's Birth 37
    The Auld Man's Fareweel 38
      to His Wee House
    On the Changes in the Habits, 40
      Amusements, and Condition of
      the Scottish Peasantry

Love and Courtship
    I'm A' Gane Wrang 54
    I Hae Lost My Love 56
    Katie Cheyne 57
    Mary Gray 71
    Some Family Correspondence 74

Humour and Satire
    Auld Ettrick John 80
    Wat o' the Cleuch 84
    The Watchmaker 88
    The First Sermon 100
    The Fortune Teller 105

The Supernatural
    Kilmeny 108
    What Is Death? 119
    A Tale of the Martyrs 122
    The Witch of Fife 132
    The Witches of Traquair 133
    The Witches' Chant 163

INTRODUCTION

The name of James Hogg tends to evoke certain standard responses: admiration, even adulation, of his great masterpiece *Confessions of a Justified Sinner*, or an admission that the reader found the work too complex, and abandoned it half-read. I belonged to the latter category for many years: it took several attempts before my mind could come to terms with that profound and troubling work (and only then after seeing a stage adaptation of it). Then there are those who reply, 'I don't know much about him, but I feel I ought to'—a circumstance brought about by a lack of low-priced texts and the aura of scholasticism which surrounds *Confessions*. There is also, frequently, surprise on learning that Hogg was the author of the lines, 'Where the pools are bright and deep, Where the grey trout lies asleep . . .' They are from 'A Boy's Song', that wonderful evocation of unsullied boyhood. To open my selection with this poem was as deliberate as the choice of a light title for the whole. For this is not a scholar's book, and I am not a scholar. I am simply an avid reader, and I regard James Hogg's poetry and prose as a 'good read'. I hope this anthology will dispel the myth that his writings are difficult, and encourage many more readers to share my enthusiasm.

I live in the valley where Hogg was born and brought up, and it may be that this background has helped me to recognize both his dialogue and his characters. But those to whom I have introduced his works over the last year have been struck, like me, with the timelessness and even the modernity of his language and ideas. To take one example: a script of 'Katie Cheyne' went astray amongst the deficiencies of the London postal service. Its unknown recipient phoned me, as my name was on it. 'I'm afraid I read it,' he said. 'It's wonderful.' He found it difficult to believe that the writer had been dead for a century and a half!

The range of Hogg's work never ceases to amaze me. Poet and songwriter—he himself wished to be seen as the heir to Burns—he was also a novelist, short story writer, essayist, and journalist. His enthusiasms spilled over into music (he played the fiddle and the flageolet) and into sport. The St Ronan's Games at Innerleithen, which he and Scott founded, still exist; and it is not beyond the stretch of the imagination to think that were he alive today he would take pleasure both in the international status of many of the sportsmen of his native Borders and in the hill races run every summer between the young men of the valleys.

One of my greatest pleasures during my year's exploration of Hogg's works was finding, in Hawick Public Library, two volumes of his plays. They are verse melodramas of differing quality but tantalizing enough to make one regret that Hogg did not pursue this form of writing. To the best of my knowledge they have never been performed. Hogg's early efforts to bring about a production came to nothing—his distrust of the actors of his day may account for this. I have included in this selection some extracts from my favourite, 'All-Hallow-Eve', and the whole of his short sketch 'Katie Cheyne'.

I have divided this anthology into four sections. They are not neat compartments: for example many of the pieces in 'Love and Courtship' are highly humourous, and 'A Tale of the Martyrs' is a story both of the supernatural and of love. The works reveal different aspects of Hogg's diverse talents, but they share a general lightness of touch and firm roots both in Hogg's life and in the countryside that formed James Hogg and created the sources from which his genius sprang.

A Shepherd's Life

Hogg's life intrigues me. It is the story of the triumph of native genius over adversity—over financial and social disadvantage and over local antipathy. The biblical quotation 'A prophet is not without honour, save in his own country' is echoed in the Border phrase of dismissal, 'Oh, him!—I kent his granny.' When James and William Hogg and their friends the Laidlaw brothers formed a literary society in the wilds of the Ettrick and Yarrow valleys, they were accused by neighbours of using their meetings to attempt to raise the devil! And, even today, in Ettrick pubs you are as likely to hear Hogg's farming and financial failures derided as his literary genius praised.

I can think of one particular parallel with Hogg's struggle to overcome his early obstacles, and that is the life of the great Danish writer Hans Christian Andersen. They were both lucky in finding the right people at the right time to remedy their early deficiencies and to understand and cope with their respective temperaments. And, like Andersen, most of Hogg's strongest works were based on the oral traditions of his youth. In his time the Dane achieved the fame that eluded the Scot; his financial position was less precarious, but Hogg was blessed with other compensations, including a happy domestic life, albeit in his fifties.

James Hogg was born in 1770 at Ettrickhall at the head of the Ettrick valley—beautiful, remote and wild. Selkirk was sixteen miles away, a four-hour ride over pitted roads. Hogg's actual date of birth is unknown. He himself believed that he was born on 25 January 1772, thus sharing a birthday with Burns. Moreover, 25 January was regarded as a 'lucky' date in the super-stitions of local folklore. Although, in his sixties, Hogg was faced with the evidence of parish records that he had been baptized on 9 December 1770, he chose to disregard this. In the Borders Regional Library there is a letter dated 25 January 1834 in which he still alludes to the date as his birthday.

His ancestors had been small farmers, the Hoggs of Fauldshope, a farm ten miles or so towards Selkirk. By the time of the poet's birth, however, their fortunes had declined, and when he was seven they were in such a state that he was forced to leave school—after less than a year's formal education—and take up cattle herding, the lowest rung in the farming ladder. His wages were a ewe lamb and a pair of boots. On his own admission he would discard the latter—and all other items of clothing—and run naked on the hills.

At school Hogg had mastered the recitation of the shorter catechism and the proverbs of Solomon. He may have learnt to read at a very basic level, but not, apparently, to write. Education need not necessarily take conventional forms however. Hogg's mother, Margaret Laidlaw (it was still customary for women to retain their father's surname after marriage), was renowned as the best ballad teller for miles around. She was forty by the time James was born, the second of four boys. She was no young inexperienced mother, but a woman with her own learning and experience to hand on to her sons. She brought them up on the tales of the countryside in which they lived: tales of the reiving times, of the Covenanters who had hidden in the hills not far distant, and above all on tales of the supernatural. Go to the upper part of Ettrick on a winter's evening, and you too will disbelieve nothing.

There was also, in the century of Hogg's birth and boyhood, another influence, one which makes the writing of *Confessions of a Justified Sinner*, with its understanding of the recesses of Calvinist doctrine, completely comprehensible. At the beginning of the century the great Thomas Boston, the most influential theologian of his day, had ministered to the parish of Ettrick for thirty years. Ettrick may have been remote, but it was a byword as a powerhouse for Boston's writings and preachings, which influenced not only Scotland but also countries as far afield as Holland and America. Boston's extremist views on the salvation of God's elect may not have found acceptance with all his parishioners or their descendants; indeed Hogg's views of religion were far from Boston's. But the minds of the so-called peasants of the area were exposed week after week to sermons of a complexity and intellectualism comparable to those emanting from, say, the faculty of divinity of a university. And the inheritance of that influence would have succeeded to the following generations—at least, I would hazard, until James Hogg's boyhood.

Hogg remained in Ettrick until his mid teens, serving a- succession of masters. At one stage he worked at Singlie, a farm about three miles from my home. During that time he bought a fiddle and taught himself to play it. According to an old diary in the possession of a present-day resident of the village, a fellow herd, one James Anderson, 'taught the Ettrick shepherd to write, sitting on a corn kist at nights'. Although Hogg does not refer directly to this incident, it does not conflict with his own accounts of his attempts at literacy. Anderson 'had his first herding at Gilmanscleuch', a farm neighbouring with Singlie, and it would seem likely therefore that Hogg, already exploring his development in one area, began to master the written word at this time. The image of the two youths, perched on a storage chest of grain, is a strong one. They call it Learning Exchange Skills nowadays, or is it Learning Skills Exchange?

But if Hogg was nurtured in Ettrick, it was in Yarrow that he blossomed. After a period of service on Tweedside, he entered in 1790 the service of the Laidlaws of Blackhouse. And yet to describe it as 'service' is to miss the whole tenor of the relationship. Mr Laidlaw was 'more like a father to me', and the whole of the educated, bookloving world in which the family lived was opened up to the young shepherd. His attempts to write verse were encouraged, and in Yarrow the shepherd became a writer.

It was in that valley, too, that he found his eventual home, through the patronage of the Duke of Buccleuch. That great patron of arts and artists granted Hogg the small farm of Altrive Lake, at a rent which was neither named nor asked for. It was there that he brought his bride in 1820, and that valley saw the remaining fifteen years of his life—domestically happy, but spurned by the critics and misunderstood by fashionable Edinburgh. He was always financially insecure, better at writing about the land than earning a living from it.

Apart from Hogg's forays into Edinburgh and periods of employment and farming ventures in Dumfriesshire, his life was spent in these two valleys. In them lie the roots of his greatness as a writer; there he knew 'a shepherd's delight'.

Life in the Valleys

Hogg never forgot what it was like to be a child and to *feel* as a child. 'A Boy's Song' captures so vividly the impressions of a country boy on a hot summer's day. The version I have chosen is that of the original manuscript; I believe the fourth stanza has never before been published.

The small hero of 'The Poachers' has his counterpart today, running wild among the litter bins and middens of the cities. The ending may be too neat, but the development of the small self-sufficient guerilla is as well observed as the countryside through which he moves.

As eternal, too, and unbounded by setting or time, is the poignant farewell of the old widower in 'The Auld Man's Fareweel to His Wee House'. There is no evidence in the poem that he is heading for the poorhouse; and indeed it is probably more likely that, like Hogg's own father, he would be spending the last of his alloted span with a son or daughter. The old man himself sees the rationale and inevitability of the move, but the desire to die amongst all that is dear and familiar is a wish all too often unfulfilled.

In that poem we see Hogg's ability to identify with a stage of life he had not yet experienced. Martha's speech to her son from 'All-Hallow-Eve' ends with the question, 'Who knows a mother's joys that has not been a mother!' Hogg was not even married by the times these lines were written, yet his grasp of a young mother's sense of inadequacy and wonder is outstanding. His country background helps explain his insight into such a situation: young mothers would suckle their babes openly while tending their flocks—a far cry from the behaviour of the drawing-room ladies of intellectual Edinburgh!

As a background to these imaginative pieces I have included an example of Hogg's journalism: a lament for the passing of the old country ways. Alas, they have been eroded still further over the centuries, though an essence of them remains. If the char-acters of the valleys about whom Hogg wrote have become adulterated over recent years by an invasion of 'incomers' such as my own family, they are nevertheless still recognizable.

Love and Courtship

Hogg's first literary successes were amongst his fellow herds and their girlfriends: love songs which were sung, to traditional airs, at kirns and social gatherings. They are delightful for their mixture of humour and lightness, their ability to catch the essence of a romantic emotion in a line or phrase. Many anthologies of love poetry contain these well-known lines:

O love, love, love!
  Love is like a dizziness!
It winna let a poor body
  Gang about his biziness!

It was through such songs that Hogg's first taste of fame came. He achieved locally the soubriquet 'Jamie the Poeter', an appellation of which he was inordinately proud. It was a collection of such songs which formed his first printed works, after the anonymously-published *Donald McDonald*, a broadsheet containing just one song.

By all accounts Hogg had a fairly active love life as a young shepherd. His friend William Laidlaw described his appearance during his Blackhouse years:

About nineteen years of age, Hogg was rather above middle height, of faultless symmetry of form; he was of almost unequalled agility and swiftness. His face was then round and full, and of a ruddy complexion, with light blue eyes that beamed with gaiety, glee, and good humour, the effect of the most exuberant animal spirits. His head was covered with a singular profusion of light-brown hair, which he was obliged to wear coiled up under his hat. On entering church on a Sunday, where he was all his life a regular attender, he used, on lifting his hat,to raise his right hand to assist a graceful shake of his head in laying back his long hair, which rolled down his back and fell below his loins. And every female eye was upon him, as, with light step, he ascended the stair to the gallery where he sat.

David Grove's anthology of Hogg's *Tales of Love and Mystery* covers Hogg's premarital adventures in some detail, so I refer the reader to that volume, and give here only a few random thoughts of my own.

The first is the incident he records in his autobiography (which remains discreet about later incidents!) of his pre-pubescent passion for Betty, a young shepherdess whom he was directed to accompany in herding at the age of eight:

Never was a master's order better obeyed . . . after dinner I laid my head down on her lap, covered her feet with my plaid, and pretended to fall asleep. . . . I wished my master, who was a handsome young man, would fall in love with her, and marry her, wondering how he could be so blind and stupid not to do it. But I thought that, if I were he, I would know well what to do.

Most of us, on reaching adulthood, disassociate ourselves from the desperate pangs of childish passion. Hogg, unafraid of them, seems to have retained a bank of emotional experiences to be re-summoned at will.

On the whole, Hogg's love poetry tends towards the self-deprecating rather than the romantically lyrical: 'I Hae Lost My Love' is a fine example of this. In 'I'm A' Gane Wrang' we see again his insight into the psychology of women, while in 'Mary Gray' (a poem published for the first time only a few years ago) humour blends most successfully with lyricism.

It is tantalizing to wonder whether or not the youthful Hogg of the Blackhouse years is personified in Duncan Stewart of 'Katie Cheyne', ready to fall in love but a lot less ready to make a commitment. At any rate, there appear to be more who claim descent from the poet than are accounted for in his genealogical tree! A clue is given in a letter written in his later years to his friend Tibbie Shiels, hostess of the famous inn. Tibbie had written to Hogg, apparently in some distress, as her son was the subject of a paternity action in the local court. In his reply Hogg advises the young man to behave as he himself had done in similar circumstances:

> I really wish Thomas would take that poor girl's child. I advise it most seriously as if I were advising my own son. Was there ever a young man disgraced by acknowledging a child? Or was there ever a man who stood out and brought it to oaths and witnesses who was not disgraced? I have taken it upon me to stop the law proceedings for the present for two very good reasons. In the first place the

examination of all the family as witnesses is going to make one of the most ridiculous exhibitions ever made in Selkirk. And in the second place after every consultation I can assure you and Thomas both that the girl's oath *will* be taken and the child sworn upon him. Therefore by all means let Thomas make as good a bargain privately with Mr [fragment missing] he can and acknowledge the child. It is the far best way of settling a disagreeable business between near relations and a way that I have chosen to do myself when sensible that the child was not mine.

I will preserve a little fodder for you of some sort but for your comfort and peace of mind and for Thomas's character I really wish he would take my advice before the law-plea be set a-going again.

Whatever Hogg's amatory adventures were, his late marriage brought him emotional stability. At fifty he found in Margaret Phillips, twenty years his junior, the perfect companion and support. The pattern of that marriage and the characters of the partners therein are thrown into sharp and recognizable focus in their correspondence. Hogg's great-grand-daughter's book *James Hogg at Home* is based on his domestic letters; from them I have selected an exchange of letters between Hogg and his wife at the end of his visit to London in 1832, when it seemed that Hogg was to be offered a knighthood. They are not passionate love letters, but they display the deep undertow of trust and lasting love between the couple, and the honesty and complete equality of their relationship. They also show the wonderful common sense of Margaret Hogg, who saw so clearly the truth of Burns's lines, 'The rank is but the guinea stamp, The man's the gowd for a' that'.

Humour and Satire

Humour creeps into most of Hogg's work, especially his prose. He cannot resist a shaft of fun. But his humour is rarely without its sharp point. Thus 'The Watchmaker', though full of comic imagery and dialogue, conveys as serious a message as any modern film against the evils of alcohol addiction.

Amongst the poems, 'Auld Ettrick John' belongs to the mainstream of Hogg's well-observed pastoral humour. 'The First Sermon', on the other hand, with its extraordinarily modern construction, is unusual for the sarcasm Hogg displays in it. Of hypocrisy and pretentiousness he says, 'Men like not this, and poets least of all'. But it is the devout countryman in him, rather than the poet, who despises these characteristics, able to compare in his mind the superior young minister of his story with the genuine pastoral care provided by the incumbments of the valley kirks.

James Hogg had a perfect ear—not just for fiddle tunes, nor just for the conversation of those around him, but for the cadences of his fellow poets. In his book *The Poetic Mirror* he parodied several of them to perfection, and it was only by a hairbreadth that the volume was not accepted as a genuine collection of the works of various poets. He captures the style of

Walter Scott perfectly in the long ballad 'Wat o' the Cleuch', part of which is reproduced here. It is a hilarious spoof of the kind of verse which Scott laboured so hard to bring to the page. We can only speculate how that great man must have received his friend's imitation!

And which of Scott's heroines would have discarded her clothing with such abandon as the wanton Maldie, whose adventures at the bracken bush are thrown back at her with such accuracy by the fortune teller in 'All-Hallow-Eve'?

The Supernatural

The resurgence of interest in Hogg in the latter part of the twentieth century is in no small measure due to a general increase of interest in the supernatural. The recent rash of paperback books, and a stream of films of the inexplicable, as well as the creation of the new Chair of Parapsychology at Edinburgh University are part and parcel of this growing trend.

Hogg grew up on tales of the 'witches, deils and fairies' of the countryside. They were not figures of fear, but rather as much a part of local lore as the natural hazards of storm or flood. Thus, in 'The Witches of Traquair' the leading witch, who may indeed have supernatural powers, is not a strange unknown figure but the hero's aunty. Hogg's own grandfather, Will o' Phaup, was reputedly the last man to have conversed with the fairies—even though his friends blamed some of his adventures on Moffat brandy!

'Kilmeny' is probably the most lyrical piece of balladry to come from the pen of any Scottish writer. It was this poem above all, part of the long *The Queen's Wake*, which established Hogg's reputation and caused such a literary sensation. That an uneducated peasant could produce such quality! Yet it was this 'uneducated peasant's' very circumstances which gave him the clear eyes that could look beyond the explainable and the rational; his imagination was untrammelled by codes and conventions. He stored in his memory the tales he had heard around him, like that of the disappearance for several days of a farmer's daughter who surfaced unharmed but unable to give an account of herself. Today a sinister or cynical interpretation would be placed on such an incident; how fortunate that a simpler society left Hogg the skeins of gold to weave into such a ballad.

'What Is Death?' is a short, previously unpublished work, the second of Hogg's 'Dramas of Infancy'. This little conversation piece between two brothers shows Hogg's understanding of the flights of fancy of innocent and free minds when faced with what is beyond their knowledge, and the forcing of such imaginings into conventional moulds by the received wisdom of their cousin.

The Covenanting 'A Tale of the Martyrs' brings to life the countryside of Dumfriesshire, where Hogg spent some time as a shepherd and in one of his unsuccessful farming ventures. The theme of the Covenanters runs through much of his prose and poetry, including, of course, his novel *The Brownie of Bodsbeck*.

The ballad 'The Witch of Fife', written in difficult, archaic Scots, is frequently included in anthologies. It is a shorter, cheerful poem of the same name which I have included here. My final choice comes again from 'All-Hallow-Eve'; the latter part has also been published as a poem in its own right.

Hogg's world of the supernatural may have had rational explanations: hysteria, hallucinogenic edible fungi—or even Moffat brandy! But it is our richness that he did not look for these human interpretations but accepted such phenomena as he accepted religion—with faith rather than awe, and without doubts. It is that clear, strong voice, accepting both the world of human frailty and the unknown powers beyond it, which rings out so truly to us across the years.

JUDY STEEL
Ettrick Bridge
1985

ACKNOWLEDGEMENTS

Douglas Mack, President of the James Hogg Society, has given most generously of his time and expertise. I am indebted to him for his guidance and suggestions, and all the help he has given, including his permission to include letters from *James Hogg at Home* by Norah Parr (Dollar, 1980).

Thanks are also due to the Librarian, Stirling University Libarary, for permission to publish texts of the following manuscripts which are contained in that library: 'A Boy's Song', 'Mary Gray', and 'What Is Death?', and to Doreen Mitchell of Henderland for allowing me to quote from the letter to Tibbie Shiel.

The staffs of the Borders Regional Library and Hawick Public Library, and Dorothy Sieber of the Archives Department, have given assistance well beyond their duties. David Groves drew my attention to the piece from the *Quarterly Journal of Agriculture*, and made many other helpful suggestions.

My publisher, Stephanie Wolfe Murray, deserves my most grateful thanks for her enthusiastic acceptance of what was no more than an idea, and for her constructive and patient help. To all these and to the many people who have encourged me—above all my husband and my young son Rory—I am most grateful.

LIFE IN THE VALLEYS

A BOY'S SONG

Where the pools are bright and deep
Where the grey trout lies asleep
Up the river and o'er the lea
That's the way for Billy and me

Where the blackbird sings the latest
Where the hawthorn blooms the sweetest
Where the nestlings plentiest be
That's the way for Billy and me

Where the mowers mow the cleanest
Where the hay lies thick and greenest
There to trace the homeward bee
That's the way for Billy and me

Where the poplar grows the smallest
Where the old pine waves the tallest
Pies and rooks know who are we
That's the way for Billy and me

Where the hazel bank is steepest
Where the shadow falls the deepest
There the clustering nuts fall free
That's the way for Billy and me

Why the boys should drive away
Little sweet maidens from the play
Or love to tear and fight so well
That's the thing I never could tell

But this I know I love to play
Through the meadow among the hay
Up the water and o'er the lea
That's the way for Billy and me

THE POACHERS

Benjamin Little, or little Benjy, as he was more generally called for a long period, was the son of a poor man of all work, who lived on the property of Sprinkell, on the Scots side of the Border. His name was Jacob. He could dress a hedge, work in a garden, mend a wheelbarrow, gird a cog, or put a gravel-walk in order. But, having no set post under his master, the baronet, he had no set wages; and for all these little odd jobs to which he was constantly putting his hand, he got literally nothing. He had one qualification, however, not yet mentioned, which was, that he could shoot a hare or black cock at any time without particular orders from the baronet. This was the cause of great trouble to him, for first one nobleman's gamekeeper found him in a transgression, then another. It is the leading principle of these men's tenets to have no mercy. They stripped Jacob of everything. They sold his split new household furniture by public auction, at his own cottage door, for ready money. Alas! it brought not one-third of its value. The eight-day clock fetched only seventeen shillings and sixpence. They sold the new blankets off the bed. They sold the bed itself; and, worst of all, they sold the double-barrelled gun for forty shillings.

This ruinous business was the death of Jacob's wife, a young creature, who had lately become the mother of a pretty boy. Whether her health was broken by reason of the loss of her bed-clothes, and her heart by the loss of her husband's effects, or by the loss of his good name, which was far worse, and which, till then, she had deemed unimpeachable,—which of these two it was, or whether it was the effect of both combined, that killed her, I do not know; but a few days afterwards, a woman named Mabel Irving called by chance on going by, and found her and her babe lying on a shakedown, in the cold corner of the empty cottage, without any covering, save a plaid and an old window-cloth. She was weeping over her unchristened boy, and called him Benoni, the son of her sorrow, blessing him with every blessing, in the name of the Lord, praying that he might be kept from the errors that had brought ruin on his hapless father, and taught to revere and keep the laws of his country, and all the while baptising him with a dying mother's tears.

The woman Irving having apprised some of the wives of the baronet's people, one of them went up to Jacob's cottage in the morning, and found poor Helen dead. She was lying pale, stretched on her lowly bed of rushes, covered with the old window-cloth, and Jacob was busy, feeding his infant boy with a soup made from a hare which he had snared for the purpose, having no other earthly thing to give him; and the little urchin seemed to be enjoying it mightily. The feelings of the country people were excited: they exclaimed against the cruelty of gamekeepers, and denounced the judgment of God on their heads; but the men defended themselves by saying that they were only doing their duty, and that if he had ceased meddling with the game intrusted to their charge, they should never have meddled with him. Jacob christened his little boy by the name of Benjamin, sent him to nurse, and continued his old practices.

His old practices, did I say? Alas! he now became ten times worse than ever! He had nothing more that the law could seize, save his person, and of that he was reckless. He contrived to buy an old gun with only one barrel, but it was a thumper. He could bring down game almost at any distance with her, and the depredations which he now made in the preserves were prodigious; and as he was grown rather a desperate character, men were not rash in meddling with him. He made a deal of money of the game, all of which he transmitted to London, so that he paid punctually for little Benjy's maintenance, but never put any furniture into his house, for fear of another seizure.

As soon as the little fellow could run about, his father brought him home to his empty dwelling, feeding him on fish and game, and taking him out poaching with him by night, to drive the hares and the game to him. When blamed for thus initiating the pretty boy so early into crime, the father said he could not help it, for he could not leave the dear little fellow sleeping by himself; and, besides, there was nothing he liked better than a bout at the hares, pheasants, and black cocks.

For the space of five or six years did the father and son and little Cocket, their dog, carry on this work of lawless depredation, and wanted for nothing; but it was a depredation so notorious as no longer to be borne: so one night as little Benjy was driving a plantation, he heard loud words and a scuffle at a distance, in the direction where he knew his father to be; and with the natural dread of an evil-doer, he hid himself in a tree. There he sat till all was again silent, and till he heard his father call his name in an under-voice; he then came down, and the two went home to their lowly couch, without any game, and as usual lay down together in the dark with little Cocket upon their feet.

Benjy was awakened at an early hour by the fierce and desperate baying of Cocket; and when the boy raised his head, he perceived that three ill-looking fellows had entered the house, and that the fury of the little pointer was keeping them at bay. Benjy only said 'Whisht, Cocket!' and the little fellow cowered down on his master's feet and ceased barking, but kept uttering an ill-suppressed growl indicative of the most heartfelt dissatisfaction. One of the men then inquired of Benjy if his father was there? He answered that he was! 'Father, here are some men wanting you,' added he; but his father made no reply.

'Oh! this is all fudge, Mr Jacob,' said they;—'a mere sham sleep, out of some evil design. Have you fire-arms beside you, rascal?' 'Ay,' said Benjy, with great simplicity. The three men then made a bolt forward to seize Jacob; but little Cocket fairly fought and beat off all the three, tearing them without mercy or mitigation of his resentment. Little Benjy now, from an internal movement of terror, tried with all his force to rise, but found himself locked to the spot; and it was not till after the most violent exertions that he disengaged himself, and when he did he was covered with one sheet of blood. When he saw this the poor fellow uttered a long cry of horror. His father was lifeless. He had died with his child clasped to his bosom; for, with all his faults, want of affection was none of them. The constables who had come to seize Jacob now retreated in dismay with the woful tidings, leaving poor little Benjy with the bloody corpse of his father. A distressed boy was he that morning: nay, he was in such a state of distraction as is scarcely to be expressed. Both his parents had now finished their lives with him in their bosoms, and both their deaths had been caused by the same crime; for poor Jacob had died of the wounds he received in the affray with the keepers the night before; and though there can be no doubt that he felt the hand of death upon him, he never mentioned the circumstance to the boy, as if unwilling to witness his distress.

Benjy now, for the first time in his life, abhorred the crime of poaching from his very soul, and resolved never more to indulge in that which had cost both his dear parents their earthly existence. Of his mother he remembered nothing, but his father had often mentioned her to him as the sweetest and most loving creature on earth, whose death was caused by those most detestable of all earthly creatures, the gamekeepers. His father he loved with a more than ordinary affection. In him and Cocket all the fond feelings of his heart were centered. He knew of no other friends, and he cared for no other; and now that he had lost the principal, his undivided affection was set on the one that remained.

Now little Cocket himself was the greatest poacher

in Scotland; not a hare, rabbit, or any game bird, could lurk within a hundred yards of his master's route, that he would not find and point as steadily as the needle to the pole. His mode was to squat close down on his belly, turn his little nose towards the game, and lie there in an agony of solicitude till his master came up. And with this little dog and a tremendous gun, called Johnnie Cope, as his sole portion, was left this poor boy, who had taken up the resolution never to poach more as long as he lived.

On the day of Jacob's funeral, poor Benjy laid his father's head in the grave, with many bitter tears and sobs that were like to rend his young heart in twain; and when the interment was over, one man thought Benjy would be going to such a place to stay, another to such another place, and the consequence was that Benjy got the offer of going to no place whatever; and not knowing where to go, he naturally, as by instinct, took the only road he had ever been accustomed to go, away to the lonely shieling at the back of the plantations. Alas! what a habitation for the poor fellow now to retire to! an empty shieling, and a lowly couch stained with the blood of his dear father! But what could he do? So he jogged slowly along, weeping as he went, and eagerly cherishing the virtuous resolution *never* to poach more, *no, never, never*, as long as he lived and breathed in the world!

As he went up by the Winter Cleuch Foot, Cocket made a dead point on the opposite brae. 'I may ay gang an' see what it is,' said Benjy to himself: 'the creature will be nae the waur o' me looking at it; and unless I spring it, Cocket will be there till the morn.' So away went Benjy across the glen to see what it was that little Cocket was pointing at so steadily. He was determined not to poach any more, but he had a stone of about half a pound weight in either hand just to throw at the creature for fun when it rose. With his arm stretched backward at its full length, ready to throw with great force, Benjy ran in on the game—turned—ran this way, and that way:—no—there was no game there, at least none that Benjy could see. Cocket still kept the point, and that so eagerly that his eyes were set in his head like the eyes of a dead creature. 'Seize him, Cocket!' cried Benjy. No sooner said than done: the word was hardly out of the boy's mouth ere the dog had hold of a great fat rabbit that had ensconced himself beneath the long grass out of Benjy's sight, and every other creature's sight; but to elude the scent of Cocket was out of his power.

How Benjy did laugh as the rabbit screamed and Cocket shook him by the throat! and when he had done worrying it, Benjy picked up his rabbit, and stroking Cocket's crown, said 'he was a little, fine, clever fellow.'

Now it is a curious fact that, as long as Jacob carried the gun, no cajoling, no pressing, could make Cocket break point and run in. For why? he well knew his master would bring the bird, or whatever it was, down, when once it was properly sprung; but when he saw his poor young master coming armed only with a stone in either hand, he took the first hint to make sure of the rabbit himself, and he contrived to play a hare the same trick before he and Benjy reached home.

There was no man in Scotland could skin and dress

a hare or rabbit more cleverly than Benjy; and what a
capital supper Cocket and he made of one of their
prizes that night! He then carried out the bloody hay,
took plenty of the sweetest-scented meadow hay he
could find into another corner of the sheiling, and
without any thing, either above or below him, save
hay, he took little Cocket in his bosom and slept
soundly till the morrow, when the sun was high up in
the east.

After a hearty breakfast, he began with a heavy
heart to look at auld Johnnie Cope. 'It was a pity to let
his father's gude auld gun gang a' ower wi' roost; he
had cleaned and oiled her oft—he wad do it again—no
that he meant to mak ony use o' her—that was out o'
the question, for the poaching had been the death o'
baith his father an' mither; but it was ae purpose like
to hae a clean thing as a dirty thing standing in a
body's house.' Thus did Benjy apostrophise himself;
and, cleaning the gun well, he set her out of his hand
with a satisfied look, quite ready for action.

He next went to his father's hidden treasure of
springes, gins, nets, and snares for every sort of game,
and surveying them all with great interest, he put a
few in his pocket; and then, purposing a walk to put
off the wearisome day, he took a long look at Johnnie
Cope, such a look as a dog takes of a morsel which he is
compelled against his will to quit. 'It couldna do
muckle ill to tak her wi' ane in case ane might fa' in wi'
a fox, or a hawk, or a glede. The country wad be weel
quat o' a wheen o' them. But then Johnnie Cope made
sic a noise through the country, an' it didna do for ane
to be making a *verra* grit noise the day after ane's

father's burial.' Johnnie Cope was actually left at home
that day; and away went Benjy and Cocket to take their
forenoon's walk.

Where do you suppose Benjy and Cocket would take
their walk that day? Of course along the highway or
some bare moor where there was no temptation, you
will say. Such were undoubtedly the most proper
places for a youth to walk who was resolved *never* to
poach more. But Benjy's walk lay through the richest
cover of the country, for he had some of his father's
old snares to lift, and some other cogent reasons for
taking that direction. He returned literally laden with
game, for, besides other shifts, Cocket seemed to
apprehend that on himself depended his master's
subsistence. Scarcely any thing could escape
him;—rabbits never did, and of these there was an
overflowing superabundance. But he likewise
frequently caught hares and black cocks, by creeping
on his belly close along the ground till within a leap of
his prey, when he very seldom missed them. Benjy
was thus naturally established as a poacher by
circumstances which he could not avert, and against
which his better judgment and feeling remonstrated.

During the day above mentioned he made a very
affecting discovery. When he went out to walk, he put
on his poaching jacket with wide tails and large
pockets, in one of which he felt something terribly
heavy thumping against his thigh: he took it out and
looked at it: it was something rolled up in a clout, and
the clout was glued together with blood. The boy
wondered; but, sitting down, he opened it, and there
was a whole hoard of guineas, more than he could

count. The poor little fellow was deeply affected, for he easily conceived that they had been placed there by the bloody hand of a dying father, the only gift that he had to bequeath to his son, whom he seems to have loved above measure. Although doubtless this was a treasure earned by the sale of game, I have always regarded it as one of the most affecting incidents I ever heard.

Day passed on after day, and week after week, and nobody seemed to regard or care for poor Benjy. He was abandoned to a lonely and lawless life; and when it was discovered that he still occupied his late father's sheiling, no sympathy was envinced for the young outlaw. In proof of this I need only relate a conversation that took place in the house of James Ferguson, one of Sir John's tenants.

'Can ony o' you tell me, sirs, what is become o' the poor fatherless an' motherless callant Benjamin Little? I am feared that creature will either dee for hunger or learn to steal.'

'As for him dying for hunger, there is nae fear o' that as long as there is game in Annandale or the woods o' Cannobie. Aih! but he is a hardened desperate wretch, and just living in the desolate cottage where his father died sae lately, an' picking up every thing o' game kind. I saw him at the guard o' the London coach wi' a box yesterday. He's gaun to the gallows as fast as he can, an' it is little matter how soon.'

'O, fie, fie, Jamie, how can ye say sae! It is a hard case to abandon a human being awthegither, without at best giving him a chance o' doing better, for as yet the poor fellow has had none. Think you he has ony sense o' religion?'

'His father Jacob had a deep *sense* o' religion, but I doubt the practice was laid aside; for how can a man who is living in the daily breach of the laws of his country engage in the ordinances of religion? He is sensible that is a mockery of both God and man, and he cannot do it. He has not the face. And as to the reclaiming o' this little rascal, that is a thing impossible, for I doubt if he kens ony mair about religion than just this—that there is a God who created man, hares, partricks, an' moorcocks, an' that his own right to these is as good as the greatest man's in the kingdom. These are Benjy's leading tenets, and he will pursue them till they bring him to his end. There's naebody feels for him, for naebody expects ony good o' him.'

When Ferguson had gone thus far, the other speaker (who was an old man, named Adam Little) went straight to Sir John, and laid the boy's case before him: the baronet instantly ordered the poor boy to be brought down to the hall and seen to, and sent to school. This was done, and Benjy left the empty house with Johnnie Cope over his shoulder, loaded, and Cocket gambolling about him. Under the guardianship of these only remaining friends, he found that he could scarcely be in bad circumstances. His gold he had hidden in the middle of a stone dike, under an elm tree, which he well knew, and in which he had often hidden game, so that Benjy felt himself rather 'an independent callant.'

But alas! in a few days it was announced to him by

the steward and gamekeeper that he must part with Cocket, who was a condemned criminal, having been caught in the preserve destroying game without mercy. This was a rending of up the last affections of Benjy's heart. He burst out a-crying, and said, he would rather part with his life than poor Cocket; he was his own, the sole friend he had on earth; and nothing but death should part them.

The gamekeeper said that then death should soon part them—the sooner the better for both; and taking out a cord, he prepared to hang up the little animal before his master's eyes. Benjy darted off like an arrow, and Cocket before him. They were pursued, and would soon have been overtaken, but Benjy had a protector for Cocket in view; and, presenting Johnnie Cope, who was loaded with swan-shot, he cocked, and then said to his assailants, 'Now touch outher me or my dog gin ye daur for the blood o' ye! I shall lay your heads where ye never shall lift them again. My dog is a treasure left me by my poor father, an' ye hae nae mair right to take him frae me than I hae to come an' take Sir John's house an' garden frae him.'

The man, perceiving the little veteran's determination in his looks, wisely kept back, and Benjy made good his retreat, keeping a sharp eye on his enemies, and his finger still at the trigger, for fear of an attack in rear.

Adam Little witnessed this scene, and could not help admiring the boy's strong affection for the little animal, as well as his undaunted resolution, and began to expostulate with the men, observing, that in his opinion they were heinously wrong and the boy was right. They answered that the separating him from that dog was the only thing that could save the poor little fellow from perdition; and for his own sake they were resolved to dispatch the dog privately, which they ought to have done at first. Old Little's heart could not approve this, and, instantly following Benjy to the shieling, he told him what he had heard, and that it was vain now to think of finding an asylum on Sir John's property on any other conditions than giving up his favourite.

Benjy said he would see them a' hanged afore he did ony sic thing; an' they had better let alone than meddle wi' him an' his dog. He wad keep possession o' his father's bit house till the neist term, in spite o' them.

Adam said that would be all fair, if he could remain there without breaking the law, which he thought very dubious; and, that he might not perish on the same rock with his hapless parents, he had resolved to take him to his sister and brother-in-law at Kirtonholm, who had no son of their own, lived beside the school, and to whom such a boy would be of great value. There he might keep little Cocket as long as he lived, and the more rabbits and hares he worried the better, for there were none in that place to find fault.

Benjy burst out into tears of gratitude; and from that moment old Little resolved to assist him with his whole protection and influence, for he saw that his heart was in the right place, and that he had a desire to be good and virtuous, if Providence would open a path for him to virtue and goodness. That night the two set out on their journey to the house of Mr Beattie, of

Kirtonholm.

This single incident in Benjy's life, his resolute defence of his little dog, changed all his circumstances, and opened to him new sources of pleasure, emulation, and ambition. He lived with Mr Beattie seven years, attending the school with his three daughters, and at the end of that period went to the college. Many wondered how he got so easily and readily through his classes, but the hoard in the bloody clout under the elm-tree helped well with that. From this store Benjy took a portion every year, and no more than what he actually needed; and many a tear it cost him when he thought of the affectionate heart that had bestowed it with that heart's last earthly throbs.

But I must hasten to the end of my simple tale. As soon as Benjy had passed his *trials*, as we say, Sir John interested himself earnestly in his fortunes, and soon procured him a living. He married his benefactor's second daughter, and there is not at this present time a more respectable presbyterian clergyman that I know of. True, on the 12th of August he is the first and deadliest shot on the moors, and the latest perhaps that traverses the bare winter fields, and beats up the bushes and hedgerows. This is accounted an aberration by some, but, at all events, it is a manly, healthy, and invigorating exercise; and to an active frame often absolutely necessary, to enable him to follow his sedentary and mental labours with energy and effect. To traverse the blooming heath swathed in the breeze of the wilderness; to look far abroad on all the goings on of nature; to bring down the black cock among his native brackens, and the moorcock on his dark and heathery waste; to mark the unerring sagacity of a favourite dog; the flights of the fowls, which, after a certain round, return always to their native spot as a place of rendezvous; to drink of the silver fountain, and rest on the flowery sward, in some lone retired fairy nook—if these are crimes, or even errors, may He whose bounty has granted us the delightful privilege forgive all who indulge in it, and among others the old Shepherd of Ettrick and the Minister of Shootinglees!

from Ackerman's Juvenile Forget Me Not *Vol. II (1831)*

GEMEL'S BIRTH

Gemel has been told by the weird women that he will die at the age of twenty-three. He asks his mother to recall the year and hour of his birth . . .

That can I well, for well may I remember!
It was that year the Kerrs and Turnbulls rode:
Thy father join'd them—Ah! that was a year
That I shall ne'er in life forget!—It was
A bloody, a severe, and stormy one!
The sheep fell down with hunger—for the snow
Lay till the suns of April master'd it.
The shepherds of the dale gather'd their dead,
And built them up for shelters to the living:
But all could nought avail!—That was a year
Not soon to be forgot—I nursed thee then
On my young breast, and sore perplex'd I was,
Not knowing how to guide thee—When I woke
I found thee often roll'd aside, and lying
Like little chubby snow-ball, sound asleep.
But nought could hurt thee—such a healthy boy,
Or happy little elf, I ne'er beheld:
When I awoke thee, thou would'st crow and smile,
And pat my bosom with thy little hand
Cold as an icicle. O how my heart
Yearn'd over thee, and clung to thee!—Who knows
A mother's joy who has not been a mother!

from All-Hallow-Eve

THE AULD MAN'S FAREWEEL
TO HIS WEE HOUSE

I like ye weel, my wee auld house,
  Though laigh the wa's an' flat the riggin';
Though round thy lum the sourick grows,
  An' rain-draps gaw my cozy biggin'.

Lang hast thou happit mine an' me,
  My head's grown gray aneath thy kipple;
An' aye thy ingle cheek was free
  Baith to the blind man an' the cripple:

An' to the puir forsaken wight
  Wi' bairnie at her bosom cryin',
My cot was open day an' night,
  Nor wanted bed for sick to lie in.

What gart my ewes thrive on the hill,
  An' kept my little store increasin'?
The rich man never wished me ill,
  The puir man left me aye his blessin'.

Troth, I maun greet wi' thee to part,
  Though to a better house I'm flittin';
Sic joys will never glad my heart
  As I've had by thy hallan sittin'.

My bonnie bairns around me smiled;
   My sonsie wife sat by me spinnin',
Aye liltin' owre her ditties wild,
   In notes sae artless and sae winnin'.

Our frugal meal was aye a feast;
   Our e'enin' psalm a hymn of joy:
Aye calm an' peacefu' was our rest;
   Our bliss, our love without alloy.

I canna help but haud thee dear,
   My auld, storm-battered hamely sheilin';
Thy sooty lum an' kipples clear
   I better lo'e than gaudy ceilin'.

Thy roof will fa', thy rafters start,
   How damp an' cauld thy hearth will be!
Ah, sae will soon ilk honest heart,
   That erst was blithe an' bauld in thee.

I thought to cower aneath thy wa',
   Till death had closed my weary e'en;
Then left thee for the narrow ha',
   Wi' lowly roof o' swaird sae green.

Fareweel, my house an' burnie clear,
   My bourtree bush an' bowzy tree;
The wee while I maun sojourn here,
   I'll never find a hame like thee!

ON THE CHANGES IN THE HABITS, AMUSEMENTS AND CONDITION OF THE SCOTTISH PEASANTRY

Chancing to be in a party of old friends the night before last, one of them gave me a touch on the elbow, and said, 'Can you tell me, Hogg, what has been the moving cause of those changes which have gradually taken place in the habits, amusements, and conditions of our peasantry, since our early recollections?'

'Upon my word, Sir,' said I, looking more than usually grave, 'the thing never struck me till this moment that you put the question; for, as having been one of them myself, and joining keenly in all their amusements for the last fifty-three years, the change has been I suppose so gradual that I never perceived it. But, on a cursory look backward, I think there *is* some difference in the characters and amusements of our young peasantry from those of a former generation; but d—l take me if I know how it has happened. Let me think about it a little while, and I'll try to account for it; for it will be a queer thing indeed if I cannot account for any thing that has taken place among the Border peasantry at least.'

'You can tell me this without any fore-thought,' said he; 'Are they worse fed, worse clothed, or worse educated than the old shepherds and hinds of your first acquaintance? Are their characters, in a general point of view, deteriorated or otherwise? Or are they more cheerful, more happy, and more devout than those of a former day?'

'In as far,' said I, 'as it regards shepherds and farm-servants, they are not in my opinion deteriorated. They are better fed, better clothed, and better educated than the old shepherds and hinds of my first aquaintance; but they are less devout, and decidedly *less cheerful and happy*.

On looking back, the first great falling off is in SONG. This, to me, it not only astonishing, but unaccountable. They have ten times more opportunites of learning songs, yet song-singing is at an end, or only kept up by a few migratory tailors. In my young days, we had singing matches almost every night, and, if no other chance or opportunity offered, the young men attended at the ewe-bught or the cows milking, and listened and joined the girls in their melting lays. We had again our kirns at the end of harvest, and lint-swinglings in almost every farm-house and cottage, which proved as a weekly bout for the greater part of the winter. And then, with the exception of *Wads*, and a little kissing and toying in consequence, song, song alone, was the sole amusement. I never heard any music that thrilled my heart half so much as when these nymphs joined their voices, all in one key, and sung a slow Scottish melody. Many a hundred times has it made the hairs of my head creep, and the tears start into my eyes, to hear such as the Flowers of the Forest, and Broom of Cowdyknows. Where are those melting strains now? Gone, and for ever! Is it not unaccountable that, even in the classic Ettrick and Yarrow, the enthusiasm of song should have declined in proportion as that of their bards has advanced? Yet so it is. I have given great annual kirns, and begun singing the first myself, in order to elicit some remnants, some semblance at least, of the strains of former days. But no; those strains could be heard from no one, with the exception of one shepherd, Wat Amos, who alone, for these twenty years, has been always ready to back me. I say, with the exception of him and of Tam the tailor, there seems to be no songster remaining. By dint of hard pressing, a blooming nymph will sometimes venture on a song of Moore's or Dibdin's (curse them!), and gaping, and half-choking, with a voice like a cracked kirk-bell, finish her song in notes resembling the agonies of a dying sow.

The publication of the Border Minstrelsy had a singular and unexpected effect in this respect. These songs had floated down on the stream of oral tradition, from generation to generation, and were regarded as a precious treasure belonging to the country; but when Mr Scott's work appeared their areanum was laid open, and a deadening blow was inflicted on our rural literature and principal enjoyment by the very means adopted for their preservation. I shall never forget with what amazement and dumb dismay the old songsters regarded these relics, calling out at every verse, 'changed! changed!' though it never appeared to me that they could make out any material change, save in 'Jamie Telfer o' the fair Dodhead.' On reading that song, both my own parents were highly offended at the gallant rescue being taken from the Elliots and given to the Scots.

With regard to all the manly exercises, had it not been for my own single exertions I think they would have been totally extinct in the Border districts. For the last forty years I have struggled to preserve them in a local habitation and a name, and I have not only effected it, but induced more efficient bodies to follow the example; such as the Great St Ronan's Border Club, the gallant Six Feet Club, &c. I have begged, I have borrowed of my rich Edinburgh friends, I have drawn small funds reluctantly from the farmers who attended, for the purpose of purchasing the prizes; but more frequently I have purchased them all from my own pocket; and though these prizes were necessarily of small value, yet by publishing annually all the victors' names in the newspapers, and the distance effected by each, and the competitor next to him, a stimulus was given for excellency in all these manly exercises, such as appears not to have existed for a century and more,—indeed, never since the religious troubles in Scotland commenced.

Still there is a change from gay to grave, from cheerfulness to severity; and it is not easy to trace the source from which it has sprung. The diet of the menials and workmen is uniformly much better than it was when I went first to service half a century ago. The tasks of labour are not more severe, but better proportioned, and more regular, and in general less oppressive. But with regard to the intercourse between master and servant, there is a mighty change indeed, and to this I am disposed principally to attribute the manifest change in the buoyant spirit and gaiety of our peasantry. Formerly every master sat at the head of his kitchen table, and shared the meal with his servants. The mistress, if there was one, did not sit down at all, but stood at the dresser behind, and assigned each his portion, or otherwise overlooked the board, and saw that every one got justice. The master asked a blessing, and returned thanks. There was no badinage or idle language in the farmer's hall in those days, but all was decency and order. Every night the master performed family worship, at which every member of the family was bound to be present, and every Sabbath morning at least, and the oldest male servant in his absence took that duty on him. The consequence of all this familiarity and exchange of kind offices was, that every individual family formed a little community of its own, of which each member was conscious of bearing an important part. And then the constant presence of the master and mistress preventing all ebullitions of untimely merriment, when the hours of relaxation came, then the smothered glee burst out with a luxury of joy and animation, of which we may now look in vain for a single specimen.

But ever since the ruinous war prices made every farmer for the time a fine gentleman, how the relative situations of master and servant are changed! Before that time every farmer was first up in the morning, conversed with all his servants familiarly, and consulted what was best to be done for the day. Now, the foreman, or chief shepherd, waits on his master, and, receiving his instructions, goes forth and gives the orders as his own, generally in a peremptory and offensive manner. The menial of course feels that he is no more a member of a community, but a slave; a servant of servants, a mere tool of labour in the hand of a man whom he knows or deems inferior to himself, and the joy of his spirit is mildewed. He is a moping, sullen, melancholy man, flitting from one master to another in hopes to find heart's ease and contentment,—but he finds it not; and now all the best and most independent of that valuable class of our community are leaving the country.

Before the revolutionary war, before a borderer would have thought of deserting his native country, he would sooner have laid down his head in the grave with his fathers, 'the rude forefathers of the hamlet.' But now all the best are leaving it; all the industrious, diligent, and respectable men who have made a little competency to carry them to another country are hastening away as if a pestilence were approaching them. God grant that it be not a prelude to approaching evil!

Again, at meal times, and in all their hours of relaxation, there are now no restraints on them as formerly. Consequently, their jokes are coarser, and one profligate servant may sometimes materially affect the probity and virtuous feelings not of one family of servants, but of many of which he is an annual member. Formerly a master and his servants rarely parted; now there is a constant circulation from one family to another throughout the whole country. The greater number of the married shepherds are, however, an exception to this. Every one of these having a share of the stock of which he has the charge, feels as much interested as his master, and is mostly a permanent possessor. These shepherds form a very intelligent and superior class of the community. But the truth is, that, for the most part, farm-servants still sustain a good name for sobriety and probity. They feel that they must do so, and that the existence of themselves and families depends on it. It is from the families of a sort of half independent class, such as feuars, that the moral quiet of the country is disturbed.

Further, if poaching may be admitted as a country pastime, there is an overwhelming increase of that of late years. When I was young, there assuredly were no game laws, or, if there were, I never heard of them. Every man who liked to take a shot did so, provided the farmers and shepherds would allow him. But there was a hard obstacle to be got over, for they would not let a man set a foot on their premises, so that in those days there were no regular or systematic poachers. There were always a few who shot a hare by moonlight, or even ventured to trace her in a snow when the farmer's stock of sheep were gathered from the hill, and that was the extent of poaching over all this country. Indeed, there were no black-cocks then. I was upwards of twenty years a shepherd ere ever I saw one in the south of Scotland, so that the temptations for poaching were not then so great. But now the poachers go forth in bands of from three to eight, with their faces blackened, their pointers and percussion-guns, and they range over the whole country from day to day, and from month to month, without once being challenged. The farmers and shepherds tried at first to stop them; but they found it both vain and dangerous. They could not seize them without a warrant, and they could not discover who they were so as to procure warrants. There is certainly something strangely deficient in the law here. I should conceive that the man who goes out among a farmer's stock, with a dog and a gun, and a blackened face, might be seized by any person concerned, and severely punished. Such a scoundrel is not tied to the killing of game alone; for it is very well known, that, in their long predatory excursions, when sometimes out for weeks at a time on the well-stocked moors, these fellows frequently pop up a lamb for their nightly fare.

As for the gamekeepers, they are the most vexatious, insolent, and insignificant persons in the whole world. If a gentleman chance to transgress by going over his bounds; or, if a farmer's friend or servant is found in a transgression; in short, whereever there is a chance of some money and eclat, in their employer's estimation, without any chance of a broken head or much trouble,—then they are amazingly active and efficient indeed, and the humbled culprit is soused with the utmost rigour of law, while the regular professed poacher is as free to the game as the first proprietor of the country. But this great annoyance is fast working its own cure. The game that a few years ago were nearly as plentiful as the sheep, and, though not a profitable stock, were certainly a beautiful one, are exhausted, and on the very eve of being totally rooted out; so that the noblemen and gentlemen have been preserving their game solely for the pleasure and benefit of the very outcasts and ragamuffins of society.

But how different were the simple amusements of

this country all the time from the close of the persecution up to the revolutionary war with France! This family union, or compact, as we may call it, between masters and servants, kept all things uniform, cheeful, and right,—for in all the sports the farmer or his family joined. The itinerant fiddlers were a great source of amusement, and a blithesome sight to many a young eye; but every farmer acknowledged one only as his family musician, and the reception of interlopers was rather equivocal. The family musician, however, knew well when to make his appearances. These were at the sheep-shearing, when he got his choice fleece; at the end of the harvest, to the kirn supper; at the end of the year, for his cakes and cheese; and at the end of seed time, for his lippie of oats. On all these occasions the neighbours were summoned, and the night spent in dancing and singing; and then, besides the farmer's bounty, it was customary for every man to give the musician sixpence, the maidens being free of every expense all over the country. But then, be it remembered, that at that period every farmer had only one farm, and his family were his principal servants; now, for the most part, every farmer has three, four, or ten of these farms, which makes the distance between master and servant wider and wider.

I have myself seen two farmers' wives, whose houses were within call of each other, meet every fine summer evening, and with their children and servants (for each of them had only a lad and lass) play a game at Blind Harry in the ewe-bught; and though I can hardly describe wherein the great sport of the game consisted, I know there was one continued yell of laughter from beginning to end of it. These moments of relaxation, during the days of the family union, had a zest in them which the menial is no more destined to enjoy.

In short, though the manly sports of the country, such as wrestling, leaping, racing on foot, putting the stone, archery, and numberless others, may, in some few places, be on the increase, still the young men have these violent exercises to themselves; and since the extermination of the penny-weddings, kirns, and family-dances, the peasantry have not an amusement in which the sexes join; and this sort of abstraction is the first thing that tends to demoralize society, and to stamp the character of man with a more rude and repulsive tint. Youth and manhood combined require some principal of excitation, and when that of female beauty is withheld from them, they must descend to a worse, the glass and boisterous mirth.

But I am far from complaining of our peasantry in this respect. A shepherd or farm-servant is rarely if ever, in this part of the world at least, found in the public-house, excepting once or twice a year, at the great fairs, when they 'tak a rouse wi' ane anither, an' wi' the lasses.' But the road-workers, young tradesmen, &c., are often loose and dissipated characters, and the public money is ill expended among them. The lasses and women folk in general would still be blithe and cheery, for their natures are constituted for it; but they have no opportunities of exercising those lively and amiable propensities, nor would they know at present how to do so if they had.

I can, therefore, only ascribe the late decided change in the character of our peasantry, *First*, to the disuse of song, arising in a great degree from the laying open to the uninitiated, our treasured and highly-valued lore of ancient minstrelsy, which lost all its interest and romance as soon as it ceased to be chanted in its native and animated lilts.

Secondly, To something radically deficient in the game laws, or in the mode of enforcing them, which I do not take it on me fully to explain or expatiate on. But I really do see no other effectual way of putting an end to this galling nuisance, except either by shooting all the game or all the poachers. It is a pity that a few regiments of them are not dispatched to Poland as sharpshooters. They would *wing* the Russians to some purpose, and certainly no class of the community could be better spared.

Thirdly, To the gradual advancement of the *aristocracy* of farming, if I may be allowed the expression, district after district being thrown into large farms, which has placed such a distance between servants and masters, that in fact they have no communication whatever, and very little interest in common. The master's eye is never upon them, and of course they have no opportunities of ingratiating themselves with him or with his family; but are subjected to all the caprices of a menial like themselves. The ancient state of vassalage was a delightful bond compared to this. It is a state of absolute slavery, with only one amelioration, namely, the liberty, at each term, of selling themselves to the highest bidder. This last, with its concomitant evils, already stated, I consider as the principal cause of the radical change which you have observed, and of which you were pleased to make the inquiries at me.'

Now, sir, I must confess that my friend did not entirely acquiesce in all these eloquent dogmas of mine, and neither perhaps will you,—but I remained obstinate as usual, and refused to retract one sentence, and so he closed the conversation by the good-natured remark, that 'there surely must be some truth in them'.

from Quarterly Journal of Agriculture
Vol. III (Feb 1831-Sept 1832)

LOVE AND COURTSHIP

I'M A' GANE WRANG

I'm a' gane wrang! I'm a' gane wrang!
　　I canna close my wakerife e'e;
What can it be that's sent this pang
　　To my young heart unkend to me?
I'm fear'd, I'm fear'd that it may prove
　　An ailment which I daurna name;
What shall I do?—if it be love,
　　I'll dee outright wi' burnin' shame!

I hae a dream baith night and day,
　　Of ane that's aye afore my e'e;
An' aye he looks as he wad say
　　Something that's unco' kind to me.
Yet love's a word my youthfu' tongue
　　Has ne'er durst utter to mysell;
I'm a' gane wrang, an' me sae young,
　　What shame for maiden's tongue to tell!

I find an aching at my heart,
　　An' dizziness that ill portends;
A kind o' sweet and thrilling smart
　　Gangs prinkling to me fingers' ends,
Then through me like a stounding pain;
　　But yet I like that pain to dree;
Then burning tears will drap like rain—
　　'Tis love, as sure as love can be!

I dinna ken what I'm to do,
   The end o' this I canna see;
I am sae young and bonny too,
   'Tis a great pity I should dee.
Yee dee I maun—I canna prove
   This tide o' pleasure and o' pain;
There's nought sae sweet as virgin's love,
   But oh, to be beloved again!

I HAE LOST MY LOVE

I hae lost my love, an' I dinna ken how,
    I hae lost my love, an' I carena;
For laith will I be just to lie down an' dee,
    And to sit down an' greet wad be bairnly.
But a screed o' ill-nature I canna weel help,
    At having been guidit unfairly;
An' weel wad I like to gie women a skelp,
    An' yerk their sweet haffits fu' yarely.

Oh! plague on the limmers, sae sly and demure,
    As pawkie as deils wi' their smiling;
As fickle as winter, in sunshine and shower,
    The hearts o' a' mankind beguiling;
As sour as December, as soothing as May:
    To suit their ain ends, never doubt them;
Their ill faults I coudna tell ower in a day,
    But their beauty's the warst thing about them.

Ay, that's what sets up the haill warld in a lowe;
    Makes kingdoms to rise and expire;
Man's micht is nae mair than a flaughten o' tow,
    Opposed to a bleeze o' reid fire.
'Twas women at first made creation to bend,
    And of nature's prime lord made the fellow;
An' 'tis her that will bring this ill warld to an end,
    An' that will be seen an' heard tell o'.

KATIE CHEYNE

Scene I

'What are ye greetin' for, Katie Cheyne?' 'I'm greetin' nane, Duncan; I wonder to hear ye.' 'Why, woman, ye're greetin' till your very heart's like to burst the laces of your gown—gie owre, for gudesake, else I shall greet too.' 'O no, Duncan Stewart, I wadna wish to see you greetin' like a wean—how can I help sobbin', when I leave my mother's house for a fremit place?' 'Keep up your heart, lass—your new place will grow like a hame, and fremit folk like sisters and brothers.' 'Well, I trust sae; what ails that wee lamb, that it bleats sae sairly, Duncan?' 'It's bleatin' for its mither; it has lost her, poor thing.' 'Can lambs like other creatures better than their mothers?' 'Na, Katie, nor half so well either.' 'O they are happy, happy creatures; but I maun gang—sae gude day.'

'Now that young simple lassie with the light feet, the blue een, the white hand, and sae little to say, had gaen' far to gaur me make a fool of myself. She maun have magic in her feet, for her light steps go dancing through my heart; and then her een! I think blue een will be my ruin, and black anes are little better; and then her tongue. "Can lambs like other creatures better then their mothers, Duncan?" The lass will drive me demented. Simple soul, now she little kenned that artless words are the best of all words for winning hearts; I think I'll step on and tell her.'

'Katie Cheyne, my dow, ye're not ill to overtake.' 'I didna like to hurt ye wi' rinnin' after me, Duncan.' 'Did ye na, Katie!—simplicity again! weel, now I like simplicity: simplicity saith the proverb,—it's nae matter what the proverb saith; but I say this, that I love ye, Katie Cheyne, wi' all my heart, and with both my hands, as the daft sang says.' 'Men are queer creatures, Duncan Stewart, an ye're ane o' the queerest o' them, and I'm no sure that I understand you. Did Jane Roden and Peg Tamson understand you, when you vowed by more stars than the sky contains that ye loved them, and loved them alone? Duncan, Duncan!' 'Hout, that was when I kenned nae better; love them, giggling hempies! I'd sooner bait a fox trap wi' my heart than send it sae gray a gate. But I am a man now, Katie Cheyne, and I like you, and liking you, I love you, and loving you, I fain would marry you. My heart's lighter with the confession.' 'And my heart's lighter too, Duncan Stewart—sae we maun e'en let twa light hearts gang thegither. But, O Duncan, this maunna be for some time yet. We maun be richer, we maun gather mair prudence; for, alas! what's two young creatures, though their hearts be full of love, when the house is empty of plenishing?' 'Now this is what I call happiness, Katie Cheyne—I'm baith daft and dizzy, but we maunna wed yet, ye say, till we get gear and plenishing. Be it sae. But now, dear Katie, ye are a simple creature, and may profit by the wisdom o' man. Take care o' yoursel in the grand house ye are gaun to. Folks there have smart looks, and sly tongues, and never put half the heart into their words that an honest shepherd lad does, who watches his flocks among the mountains, with the word of God in his pocket, and his visible firmament above him. Be upright, and faithful, and just towards me; read at spare times, in your bible; and beware of those creatures whose coats are of divers colours, and who run when the bell rings.' 'Ay, and take ye care of the ewe-milking lasses, Duncan. There will be setting on of leglins, and happing wi' plaids, and song-singing, and whispering when Katie Cheyne's out o' sight. But whenever you see ripe lips and roguish een, think on me, and on our solemn engagement, Duncan Stewart.' 'Solemn engagement! the lass has picked that out o' some Cameronian sermon. It sounds like the kirk-bell. I shall set ye in sight of your new habitation, and then farewell till Lammas fair.'

Scene II

'Weary fa' thee, Duncan Stewart. Solemn engagement! what a serious sound there is in the very words. I have leaped o'er the linn wi' baith een open. I have broken my head wi' my ain hand. To be married is nothing, a light soke is easily worn, and a light yoke is easily borne. But I am worse than wedded, I am chained up like a fox amo' chickens, tied like a hawk amo' hen birds—I am fastened by a solemn engagement, and canna be loosed till siller comes. I maun gang to kirk and market wi' an antenuptial collar about my neck, and Katie Cheyne's name painted on't, and all who run will read. I'll never can face Peg Tamson nor Nell Rodan; they'll cry, "There gangs poor Duncan Stewart, the silly lad, that is neither single nor married." I like nae lass half sae weel, but then it's the bondage o' the solemn engagement: who would have thought such a simple creature could have picked up twa such lang-nebbit, peacock-tailed words? Hoolie, Duncan! here comes thy mother.'

'Duncan! son Duncan! you are speakin' to yersel'. No young man ever speaks to himsel' unless he is in love.' 'An' what an I be, dear mither, there is nought unnatural in the situation.' 'Love, my son, is natural only when fixed on a proper object; you have good blood and high blood in your veins, and if you look low, you will lift little. Keep your mother's house in remembrance.' 'I never thought a thought about it. I ken ye were a lady, for ye have aye said sae, but simple blood hauds up a poor man's roof-tree, while gentle blood pulls it about his lugs.' 'Lugs! O that son of mine should utter that vulgar word! O that a descendant of the ancient and honourable house of Knockhoolie should speak the language of plebeian life! How will you speed in your wooing with your fair cousin of Glenpether, if you are guilty of such vulgarisms? How will a man enter with dignity upon her fair possessions, seven acres of peatmoss and a tower with a stone stair—who says, "Lugs"?' 'O mither, mither, it's all over, all these grand visions maun vanish now; I am not my own man, I am settled, tied up, tethered, side-langled—I am under a solemn engagement.' 'What! has a son of Knockhoolie wedded below his degree? O that shame should ever fall on an ancient house—on a house whose dowry is a long descent and spotless honour—on a house that's as good as related

to that of Pudinpoke, one of the most ancient names
in the south country. Duncan Stewart, there has been
Knockhoolie in Knockhoolie longer than tongue can
tell or history reckon.' 'Married! mither, marrying's
nought, it's but a shoot thegither o' twa foolish things,
by a man mair foolish than either. But I'm contracted,
bespoke, gi'en awa'; I'm no my ain man, I'm the slave
o' a solemn engagement; heard ye ever sic binding and
unlooseable words? And wha wad hae thought that a
simple quean, like Katie Cheyne, would have had such
words in her head?' 'Solemn engagement, my son;
these are looseable words, keep the enchantment of
the law, and the spell o' pen and ink away from them.
But Katie Cheyne! a lassie who has never heard of her
grandfather, a creature dropped like a flower seed in a
desert, is she decreed to give an heir to the house of
Knockhoolie?' 'O mither, I'm a born gowk, a
predestined gomeral, and doomed to be your sorrow.
O can wit or wise words loose me? Try your hand, but
be not severe with the lassie, for she's a simple lassie.
Slide cannily into the leeside o' her good opinion, and
slip this antenuptial halter out o' her hand; and then I
shall gang singin' wi' a free foot owre the hill to my
cousin o' Glenpether.' 'Spoken like thy mother's son!
O that you had ever such a sense of your born dignity!
O that you would leave off the vulgar pursuits of the
quoits, and pitch the bar, and hap, step, and loup, and
learn to speak the language of polished life. Learn to
think much and say little, and look as if you knew
every thing, so that the reputation of wisdom might
remain with the house of Knockhoolie.'

Scene III

'Well, mither, what says Katie? O the simple slut! O
the young uninstructed innocent! "Can lambs like
other creatures better than their mothers, Duncan?"
She's as sweet as a handful of unpressed curd, and as
new to the world as fresh kirned butter. But solemn
engagement; what says she to the solemn engagement?' 'Little, Duncan, very little; first she put one
hand to her eye, and then another, and at last said. "He
made it, and he may undo it, but I maun hae his ain
word for't, for mithers are mithers, and may be
wilfu'."' 'O then, I have got this matrimonial hap-
shackle off, and am free. Losh, how light I am! I think I
have wings on. Now I can flee east, and flee wast, here
a word and there a word, step afore the lasses as crouse
as a cock wth a double kame on. I'll make them sigh at
their suppers.' 'You have reason, my son, to be lifted
up of heart, ye can now act as becomes your mother's
house. What colour had your cousin of Glenpether
when ye steppit ben wi' the kind word and the well-
bred bow?' 'Colour! just the auld colour, a kind o' dun
and yellow. But ye see there was a great deal of
blushing and snirting, and bits o' made coughs, as if to
keep down a thorough guffaw. I have nae notion o'
courting ladies.' 'Tell me, Duncan, how you demeaned
yourself, and how your cousin received you.' 'That's a
lang story, mither, and a misred ane. I rappit an' I
whistlet, and wha should come to the door but a dink
and sonsie lassie, ane Bell Macara. "Is Miss Mattie at
home?" says I; "Deed is she," says the lass, as nice a
lassie as well could be. So ye think, mither, that Katie

Cheyne will free me?' 'No doubt of it, Duncan, my child; well what next?' 'Weel, this Bell Macara says to me—I wish you had seen her, mother, a quean wi' spunk and smeddum, and then her tongue, says Bell, says she, "Yes, sir, she is at hame, will ye walk into the kitchen till I inform her?" The kitchen, thinks I, is a step beneath me, however she gied me sic a look, sae into the kitchen went I, shoulder to shoulder wi' Bell Macara.' 'O son Duncan, ye will break my heart: a kitchen wench, and you a son of the house of Knockhoolie!' '"If you are not in a hurry, sir,"' says Bell Macara, "I have a bakin' o' bread to put to the fire." "I *am* in a great hurry," says I. "No doubt on't," said she, "sir"—she aye sirred me, "they are aye in the greatest haste that hae least to do." She's a queer weelfaur'd quean now, this Bell Macara, and has a gift at haurning bread.' 'Son, son, tell me what passed between you and your lady cousin, or hold your peace forever.' 'O but I maun relate baith courtships, for that ane has a natural reference to the other.' 'Both courtships! Have you courted both maid and mistress?' 'Mither, mither, be reasonable now, if ye ever saw a lass, bonnie belike, skilful wi' her een, mischievous wi' her tongue, spreading out a' her loveliness before ye, like Laird Dobie's peacock's tail.' 'How, Duncan, can ye speak so to me, one of the daughters of the house of Knockhoolie?' 'Daughter! ay! but had ye been ane o' its sons! Or, what would please me better, were you as young as ye hae been, and as well-faur'd, wi' an auld-farrand tongue, and twa een that could look the lark out o' the lift, and you to meet a pleasant lad, wi' love strong within him, ah, mither!' 'My dear son, my dear son, why remind me of other days? let all byganes be byganes.' 'There now, I kenned nature would speak, in spite of you: and was I to blame for an hour's daffin' wi' bonnie Bell Macara? I am free to own, but a man canna help his nature, I have a wonderfu' turn for fallin' in love. So, says Bell Macara to me—this was the hinderend of all, says Bell to me, "If ye miss a kind reception up stairs, ye may come down again, and gie a poor body a fleein' bode." "There's my thumb on't," says I; and I walked up stairs wi' her, hand for hand. Then, ye see, she opened the door o' my lady cousin's room, and cried out, "Mr Duncan Stewart, ma'am, from Knockhoolie;" and in I gaed, my bonnet in my hand, my best plaid wrapped about me, wi' beck and wi' binge, lookin' this way and that way.' 'Duncan Stewart, are ye ravin', a grey plaid, and becking and binging! had you both your dogs with you?' 'I wish they had been, poor dumb creatures; but I did my best without them. Bell Macara lookit at my cousin, and my cousin at Bell Macara—that queer kind of look when, without speaking, lasses say sic a ane's a sumph, or sic a ane's a sensible fallow. Now Bell Macara's twa een said, "He's a comical chap, he's no a made up frae the pan and spoon." "Be seated, cousin Duncan," said my cousin to me; and down she sat on the sofa, and down clinked I beside her. "Sit still, Mattie," says I, "for I have some queer things to say." "Say away," she says, "what would ye say?" "I'm no certain yet," quoth I, "what I'm going to say; but I ken brawly what I'm going to do." And afore she either kenned or cared, I had nearly given her a hearty smack that wad hae done her heart gude.'

'Ha! ha! well done, Duncan. It was a bold and downright way of beginning to woo, but ladies of our blood love the brave and the bold, though I know such strong measures are opposed by many ladies of quality. Nevertheless, I approve, get on; how did she take it?' 'Just middling, she reddened up, called me rude, forward, country-bred, till I was obliged to try my lip on her cheek again, and that sobered her.' 'Well, Duncan, well, but you should not have been quite so audacious. Men never pity woman's softness, but are rude in the sight of the world.' 'Na, mither, na,—I threw my plaid o'er her, and under that pleasant screen, e'en put it to my cousin if she could like me;—me rude afore the world! I ken better than that.' 'There's hope o' you yet my son; and what said the young lady?' 'Young lady! nane sae young, five and thirty, faith! Says she to me, "I hate plaids." "Ye hate plaids," says I; "that's queer." "No sae queer either," said she, "for they make us do things we would never have the face to do without them." "O blessings on the shepherd's plaid," cried I, "it haps us frae the storm, it is the canopy of kindly hearts; many a sweet and soft word, many a half unwilling kiss, many a weel fulfilled vow have passed under it. The een o' malice canna glance through it, the stars nor the moon either; it's a blessed happing." "Ye had better, as ye havena far to gang to grow daft, break into song at once," said our cousin. "Thank ye,' said I; and I sang sic a sang, ane made o' the moment, clean aff-loof, none of your long studied, dreigh-of-coming compositions. Na! na! down came the words wi' me, with a gush like a mill shelling. I have verse the natural gate, and ither folk by inoculation. I sang such a song; listen now:—

> My blessings on the cozie plaid,
>   My blessing on the plaidie;
> If I had her my plaid has happ'd
>   I'd be a joyfu' laddie.
>
> Sweet cakes an' wine with gentlemen
>   All other fare surpasses,
> And sack and sugar wi' auld wives,
>   But bonnie lads wi' lasses.
>
> O for a bonnie lad and lass—
>   And better for a ladie,
> There's nought in all the world worth
>   The shepherd's cozie plaidie.'

'Really, Duncan, my dear son, there is a rustic glibness about the verses, but do not give up your mind to so common an acomplishment. What said your cousin?' '"Pray favour me with the chorus," said she; "I am fond of choruses." "This is the chorus," said I, and I tried my lip; but aha! she was up—had been disciplined before. "Off hands," quoth my cousin, "and sit at peace till my father comes; else I shall ring for Bell Macara to show you to your own room, where you may cool yourself till my father comes home." "Do sae," says I, "do sae, I have no objection to the measure, if Bell bears me company:" so I offered to ring the bell, thinking there would be some fun in the change. "Stay," said my lady Mat, "stay," said she, and she laid her hand on mine—"I was going to observe," said she, "that Bell Macara is a superior girl." "I think so too," says I; "shall I ring for her?" "No," says my cousin; "all that I was going to say was that Bell is a good-looking young woman." "I told her sae," says I, "no an hour since. She is a thrifty girl, and a hard-working—she bakes bread weel," said I. "She has a very fine eye," said my cousin. "Twa o' them," said I, "and shiners." "Well then, she would make you a capital wife," says Mattie to me. "Would she?" said I: "I wish ye had told me sooner, for I am in a manner disposed of; a woman has a kind o' property in me, I have come under a solemn engagement. Have ye never heard that I am to be married to a certain saucy cousin o' my ain, a great heiress, who has broken the hearts o' three horse-coupers wi' drinkin' her health in brandy?" "And who is this fair cousin o' yours?" says Miss Mattie to me: "I never heard of such a matter." "That's queer again," said I, "for my mither has talked of it, ay, and she can talk, she talks nought but the wale o' grand words, born gifts, born gifts, and we should na be vain. But, as I said, my mither has talked, and I have talked, and the thing's next to certain." "But," said my cousin, "name her, name her, ye havena mony cousins, and they all have names." "And this ane has a name too," says I; "but she's no that young, and she's no very bonnie; but the pretty acres about her are the thing. She's rich, and ripe, and disposed to be married." "Now," said she, and her rage nearly reddened her yellow complexion, "this is some of your mother's idle dreams. She sits building palaces of the imagination. Go and tell her from me, that, though I am *auld*, and *ugly*, and *rich*, and *disposed to be married*, I am no a fool. I'm no sae simple a bird as to big my nest with the gowk."

'I never loot on I heard her. "But my cousin," says I, "has a waur fault than lack o' beauty, she has a fine gift at scolding, and she rages most delightfully. I maun take her through—canna draw back." "Duncan Stewart," cried she, "begone! Never shall your cousin give her hand to such a lump of God's unkneaded clay as you—never connect herself with folly, though she is *disposed* to be married. Could I wed a clown, and see his mad mither sitting next me at my table?" "Who was talking o' your table?" says I; "the table will be mine, and next me shall my ain auld mither sit. But sit down, Mat, my lass, dinna rin awa." I trow I answered her.' 'You behaved very well, my dear Duncan, very well considering. I scorn her personal insinuations. Alas! the children of this generation have not the solid qualities of those of the last. You have other cousins, Duncan, my son; cousins with land and houses, who love your mother for her mind and her sense of family dignity. Ye must not lay a dog in a deer's den; ye must always lay out your affections on birth and breeding.' 'My father was a shepherd, mither, spelt the bible as he read it, drank hard at clipping-time and lambing-time, when the heather was in blossom and when the snaw was on the ground. Was he a man o' birth and breeding?' 'Duncan, I doubt ye are incapable of comprehending the feeling which influences those of ancestry and elevation of soul. I married your father for his good sense and good taste, *he* never made love to low-bred maidens.' 'An excellent apology for all manner of marriages, mither. Bell Macara, now, is a lass o' taste, and so is Jenny Ste'enson, and poor Katie Cheyne has the best taste of a'; but I hae shaken mysel' free o' Katie—I wrote her such a letter, ye never saw such words, it will drive her to dictionar' and grammar, ne'er ane o' less length than her ain words "solemn engagement," and high sounding as "tremendous." They were all nice, long-nebbit words, and I'm only afraid mither, I'll awa' to Kate Cheyne—its time I were awa'.' 'Truly is it, Duncan, and of that I am come to speak; she bids you to her bridal. She is to be wedded at twelve o'clock, to a man of her own degree, Colonel Clapperton's grieve, Jock Hutcheson—Jenny Davidson's Jock—like aye draws to like.' 'Jock Hutcheson, mither,—what! lang Jock Hutcheson—that can never be! He's naebody, ye may say—lang, and black, and tinkler-looking—and has thrashen me twenty times—it canna be him.' 'But it is him, Duncan, and glad I am of it; so get down the saddle wi' the plated stirrups—the silver's sore gone—still they *were* plated—and catch the horse on the common, wisp it down, and ride like your ancestors of old—cock your bonnet, and wag your arm manfully.' 'Mither, I'll be married too—married I shall be—married if there's a willing lass in the country side, and as muckle law in the land. Married I *shaal* be—I'm as fixed as Queensberry, as Criffel, as Skiddaw-fell—O for the names of more mountains!' 'Duncan, dear Duncan, be guided; are ye mad?' 'Yes, I'm mad; d'ye think the marrying fit would ever come on me unless the mad fit came afore it?' 'Now then, my son, be ruled, throw not away the last child of an ancient line on nameless queans; wed in your degree. It would be a pity to see an old inheritance like mine going to children of some lass whose kin cannot be counted.' 'It's easy talking, mither; will a born lady, wi' as muckle sense as a hen could haud in her steekit nieve, tak' Duncan Stewart? I maun marry them that will marry me. I hear the trampling of horses.' 'Horses, ay, here's horses—here's your full cousin Grizel Tungtakit of Tungtakit, riding on her galloway nag away to Kate Cheyne's penny-wedding, with her lang riding habit and her langer pedigree. She's a perfect princess, and come to the years of discretion—wi' a colour in her cheek to stand wind and rain. Take her, Duncan, take her!—she's lady of Tungtakit; a fair inheritance—feeds six ewes in a dropping year. Take her, Duncan, take her!' 'Tak' her! no, an she were heiress of all the sun shines on. Take *her!* she has a heart that wad hunger me, and a tongue that wad clatter me to death. Cousins are closers, mither,—cousins are closers—the mad fit o' wedlock's more composed sin' ye spak! I think I may shoot owre till winter. I wadna thought o' marrying at a' if that daft hempie Kate Cheyne hadna put it into my head. I'll owre the hill to the Elfstane Burn, and grip a dizen o' trouts for our dinner, and let the bridal train ride by. I wonder if Kate will be wedded in her green gown—and if Jock Young of Yetherton will be best man?'

MARY GRAY

When the last beam o' the day
  Down the westlin hill had gane
When the mist was on the brae
  An' the moon was in wane
Wi' my cosy plaid o' gray
  An' my doggie at my heel
I gaed a weary way
  But I kend it weel

The heathcock on the fell
  Wi' his gollar loud an' deep
He made a' the cleughs to yell
  An' made a' my hair to creep
For I thought he seemed to say
  In anger an' a fret
Ha Jock how dare ye gae
  Tae the courtin sae late

The bleat of the curlew
  Frae the grey an' lonely waste
An' the plover's eiry whew
  Came across me the neist
An' ilk ane seemed to cry
  On my Mary mournfullye
As if grief were drawing nigh
  An' the blame lay wi' me

I saw a bogle here
  An' I saw a bogle there
In the lang unfarrant claes
  That the bogles wont to wear
But my Bawtie cocked his tail
  An' gaed trottin' without fear
An' I kend that naught unrale
  Or unearthly was near

For my Bawtie kens as weel
  A bogle frae a drain
Frae a scar upo' the hill
  Or fearsome auld gray stane
As I could ken a rae
  Frae the brocket o' the hind
Or my bonny Mary Gray
  Frae a' womenkind

Poor Bawtie wan the door
  But he couldna get in
Sae he scrapit wi' his foot
  And my Mary kend the din
An' she opened cannilye
  An' she clapped his honest brow
Ha Bawtie are you there
  An' nane there but you

I keekit sleely in
  To see what I could see
An' saw the saucy brute
  Sitting fawnin at her knee
An' he gae her ay a paw
  An' he lookit to the door
An' weel she kend the sign
  She had seen oft afore

I gat a wee bit flyte
  For a late untimely guest
An' keeping fo'ks awake
  Wha had muckle need to rest
But lang ere it was day
  There I gat a dear propine
For my bonny Mary Gray
  Had own'd her heart was mine

Some say we shouldna gang
  To the lasses late at e'en
Lest something should gae wrang
  Or some awsome thing be seen
But nae pleasure o' this earth
  Will I e'er compar beside
The lassie o' ane's heart
  At her ain ingle side

SOME FAMILY CORRESPONDENCE

Waterloo Place March 10th

Dearest Margt

I send you a single line merely to say that I am very well and that I never had my health better now that I think I shall be home with you about the end of the month or the first week of the next but I shall write before leaving London. I am quite sick of it. You know I was always fond of flattery and approbation but I have at length lived to be overpowered with it and thought it would be all your interests that I should remain here I feel I must leave everything and return to the bosom of my family and though very little richer than when I left you still I have set things in motion. I got a public dinner from the great Walton-Cotton club yesterday was made an honorary member and decorated with the order. You must consult your own heart whether you would like to be Lady Hogg or remain the Ettrick Shepherdess because you may now have the former title if you please. The Queen is it seems intent on it and I got a letter the other day from Lord Montagu requesting me not to see his Majesty until he and I consulted together as he understood there was some risk of being knighted which would run me into the expense of at least £300: of fees. For my part I despise it in our present circumstances and can see no good that it could do to us. It might indeed introduce our family into the first ranks but then where is £300: to come from. In short I want you to dissuade me from it but I'll not look near his Majesty till I hear from you so write me directly. Dr Brewster was knighted yesterday. The cholera is raging and spreading terribly here now but do not say a word about that to James else it will kill him. How I am longing to have you all one by one in my arms again Bestow a benediction on every one of our dear dear children in their father's name and kiss each of them for me.

Your very affectionate husband
James Hogg

to Jas Hogg Esq. 11 Waterloo Place London
Altrive Lake March 15th 1832

My ever dearest James

From my heart I can say I like no such titles & if you value your own comfort & my peace of mind you will at once, if offered to you, refuse it, it is an honor you may be proud to refuse but not to accept I think a title to a poor man is a load scarcely bearable, I daresay there are many men born with one on their back who would be thankful if they could to get rid of it, Her Majesty must be entirely ignorant of your circumstances if the thing has *really* ever been thought of. So I hope if you are to have an interview with their Majesties, you will in your own short pithy way express your gratitude for the honor they intended to confer upon you assuring them you know they wish you well but from prudent reasons you must decline the offer, did I posssess five thousand a year I should wish to be unencumbered with a title I want no more than to be the wife of plain James Hogg, we ought to consult the happiness of our family & such a thing I should look upon in every respect would be to them in all probability great misery. I could say a thousand against it, did I consider it at all necessary but not doubting for a moment your seeing the impropriety of it shall say little more only I must say should you come back with such a burden on your back you will return infinitely poorer than when you left me suppose you were to add hundreds to your income—Thank God we are all well except Jas who has been complaining for some time he is seldom two days well at one time yet he is better than he has been & I flatter myself when you return he will get quite well he is very tall & looks rather delicate he has not been at school for a month of course has made little progress in his learning since you left he gets lessons at [?home] but he is not as hearty in the cause as we could wish. Dear little Mary was inoculated on Saturday & appears to be doing well Mr Anderson I expect back in the end of the week to see her—all the children Mr B and myself are wearying terribly for you to come back do I beseech you come immediately you have already been 3 months away from us. Should you be at the Palace take good notice for I should like to hear about our good King & Queen & consult Lord Montague or some other prudent friend as to your dress I should wish you to appear as plain as possible to be consistent with the place—

I have settled so far a number of little accts. all unasked

for & am trying to get the house forward the wood is got & the passage is to be opened up very soon—Come in the end of the month really I feel great anxiety about you at this time May God be with you & preserve you in health—I think you had better come by land though it is more expensive I see by the news papers Cholera has been in some of the London packets write before you leave Lond—if you come by Selkirk I shall get a Gig & send to meet you— As I hope to see you soon I shall finish this letter

Your ever affect
M Hogg

[in a childish hand]

My dear Papa

I have not been well since you left us but I think I shall get well when you come home now dear Pappa come this month—your affect son

Jas Hogg [aged 11]

11 Waterloo Place March 23rd 1832

My beloved Margt,

Your last has fairly upset my resolution of remaining here any longer my dear boy's health being far dearer to me than either honour or riches of course I shall neither see the King nor Queen. I called on the Duke of Buccleuch yesterday but find that he will not arrive here before the 28th so I shall not see him either but I will call again on Lord Montague. I dine again with the

Highland Society to night and shall meet with many of the first nobles of the land this being their great anniversary. I leave London to morrow evening and sail for Edinr on Sabbath morning in the United Kingdom steamship which never takes above fifty-two hours at farthest in a trip, so that I shall be in Edinr in all probability on Tuesday the 27th where at Mr Watson's I shall be happy to meet with you and Mary and Harriet or if you cannot possibly get away you might send Peggy with her. I will buy her a new hat and any thing she needs there. If you do not meet me I will make as little stay in Edinr as possible but haste home. I am positively worried with kindness so that I do not know what to do first and I positively will not come to London again without you. I am in excellent good health and

> Your ever affectionate husband
> James Hogg

from James Hogg at Home *Norah Parr (Dollar 1980)*

HUMOUR AND SATIRE

AULD ETTRICK JOHN

Air—Rothiemurchie's Rant

There dwalt a man on Ettrick side,
    An honest man I wat was he;
His name was John, an' he was born
    A year afore the thretty-three.
He wed a wife when he was young,
    But she had dee'd, and John was wae;
He wantit lang, at length did gang
    To court Nell Brunton o' the Brae.

Auld John cam daddin' down the hill,
    His arm was waggin' manfullye,
He thought his shadow look'd nae ill,
    As aft he keek'd aside to see;
His shoon war four punds weight a-piece,
    On ilka leg a ho had he,
His doublet strang was large an' lang,
    His breeks they hardly reached his knee;

His coat was thread about wi' green,
   The moths had wrought it muckle harm,
The pouches were an ell atween,
   The cuff was fauldit up the arm;
He wore a bonnet on his head,
   The bung upon his shoulders lay,
An' by its neb ye wad hae read
   That Johnnie view'd the milky way:

For Johnnie to himself he said,
   As he came duntin' down the brae,
'A wooer ne'er should hing his head,
   But blink the breeze an' brow the day;'
An' Johnnie said unto himsel',
   'A wooer risks nae broken banes;
I'll tell the lassie sic a tale
   Will gar her look twa gates at ance.'

But yet, for a' his antic dress,
   His cheeks wi' healthy red did glow;
His joints war knit and firm like brass,
   Though siller-gray his head did grow;
An' John, although he had nae lands,
   Had twa gude kye amang the knowes,
A hunder punds in honest hands,
   An' sax-an-thretty doddit ewes.

An' Nelly was a sonsie lass,
    Fu' ripe an' ruddy was her mou',
Her een war like twa beads o' glass,
    Her brow was white like Cheviot woo;
Her cheeks war bright as heather-bells,
    Her bosom like December snaw,
Her teeth was whiter nor egg-shells,
    Her hair was like the hoody craw.

John crackit o' his bob-tail'd ewes;
    He crackit o' his good milk-kye,
His kebbucks, hams, an' cogs o' brose,
    An' siller out at trust forby;
An' aye he showed his buirdly limb,
    As bragging o' his feats sae rare,
An' a' the honours paid to him
    At kirk, at market, or at fair.

Wi' sic-like say he wan the day,
    Nell soon became his dashin' bride;
But ilka joy soon fled away
    Frae Johnnie's canty ingle side;
For there was fretting late an' air,
    An' something aye awanting still:
The saucy taunt an' bitter jeer—
    Now, sic a life does unco ill.

An' John will be a gaishen soon;
   His teeth are frae their sockets flown;
The hair's peel'd aff his head aboon;
   His face is milk-an'-water grown;
His legs that firm like pillars stood,
   Are now grown toom an' unco sma';
She's reaved him sair o' flesh an' bluid,
   An' peace o' mind, the warst of a'.

May ilka lassie understand
   In time the duties of a wife;
But youth wi' youth gae hand in hand,
   Or tine the sweetest joys o' life.
Ye men whose heads are turning gray,
   Wha to the grave are hastin' on,
Let reason a' your passions sway,
   An' mind the fate o' Ettrick John.

Ye lasses, lightsome, blithe, an' fair,
   Let pure affection win the hand;
Ne'er stoop to lead a life o' care,
   Wi' doited age, for gear or land.
When ilka lad your beauty slights,
   When ilka blush is broke wi' wae,
Ye'll mind the lang an' lanesome nights,
   O' Nell, the lassie o' the Brae.

WAT O' THE CLEUCH

Wat o' the Cleuch came down through the dale,
In helmet and hauberk of glistening mail;
Full proudly he came on his berry-black steed,
Caparisoned, belted for warrior deed.
Oh, bold was the bearing, and brisk the career,
And broad was the cuirass, and long was the spear,
And tall was the plume that waved over the brow
Of that dark reckless borderer, Wat o' the Cleuch.

His housing, the buck's hide, of rude massy fold,
Was tasselled and tufted with trappings of gold;
The henchman was stalworth his buckler that bore;
He had bowmen behind him and billmen before:
He had Bellenden, Thorleshope, Reddlefordgreen,
And Hab o' the Swire, and Jock of Poldean;
And Whitstone, and Halston, and hard-riding Hugh,
Were all at the back of bold Wat o' the Cleuch.

As Wat o' the Cleuch came down through the dale,
The hinds stood aghast and the maidens grew pale;
The ladies to casement and palisade ran,
The vassals to loop-hole and low barbican,
And saw the bold Borderers trooping along,
Each crooning his war-note or gathering-song:
Oh, many a rosy cheek changed its hue,
When sounded the slogan of Wat o' the Cleuch!

As downward they passed by the Jed and the Roule,
The monk took his crosier, his cord, and his cowl,
And kneeled to the Virgin with book and with bead,
And said Ave-Maria and muttered his creed,
And loudly invoked, as he clasped the rood,
Saint Withold, Saint Waldave, Saint Clare, and
    Saint Jude:
He dreaded the devil, to give him his due,
But held him as nothing to Wat o' the Cleuch.

Wat o' the Cleuch he lighted down;
He knocked at the gate, but answer had none;
He knocked again with thundering din,
At length he heard a stir within.
'Who raps so loud?' a voice 'gan cry;
'Swith! open the door,' said Wat, "tis I.'
Then some ran here, and some ran there,
They whispered and muttered words of prayer:
'Come quick!' cried Wat, and then
The door was oped by an abbot old,
With bushy beard and ronkled mould,
Who scarce could tears restrain:
Oh, how he groaned and heaved the sigh
As the stark and stalwart chief strode by!
And if his prayer then we knew,
'Twas not for grace to Wat o' the Cleuch.

Wat deigned no heed, but onward strode
To the chancel of the house of God:
He threw up his visor and helm to boot;
He wiped his brow and looked about,
And fixed his eye on where a crowd
Of haggard friars trembling stood;
Then in deliberate way
His mighty two-hand sword he drew;
'Twas broad and long, but of a hue
Ill suited fears to stay.
For segments deep of blackened red
Its polished side half covered,
As if half-way through many a head
It late had found its way.

*   *   *

Wat gave his sword a swing behind;
It whistled in the convent wind
With ireful sound, and by ill luck
Against the architrave it struck,
Just where Saint Peter held the key
Forth to the sainted Gregory.
Down came th' apostle from the wall,
The pope, the key, and pedestal.

Wat looked behind, he looked before,
And, prostrate on the convent floor
Beheld the canonized compeers,
Amid their rueful worshippers:
Longer the scene he could not brook,
He laughed till all the rafters shook.

THE WATCHMAKER

David Dryburgh was the head watchmaker in the old burgh of Caverton, and a very good watchmaker he was; at least I never knew one who could better make a charge, and draw out a neat and specious bill. Every watch that went to him to clean required a new mainspring at least, and often new jewels for pivots to the fly-wheel, or a new chain or hairspring; or, if the owner had a very simple look, his watch needed all these together.

But experience teacheth fools wisdom. David, for all his good workmanship and handsome charges, never had one sixpence to polish another; so, after due consideration, he said to himself one day, 'This will never do! I must have a wife! There is no respectability to be obtained in this world without a wife! No riches, no comfort, without a wife! I'll have one, if there is one to be had in this town for love or money. Money! God bless the mark! I'll not have a lady. No, no; I'll not have a lady; I never could find out what these creatures called ladies were made for. It could not be for mothers of families, for not one of them can nurse a child; and it is a queer thing if our Maker made so many handsome elegant creatures just to strum upon a piano, eat fine meat, an' wear braw claes. No, no! Before I married a lady, I would rather marry a tinkler. I'll marry Peg Ketchen. She can put a hand to every thing; and if any body can lay by something for a sore foot or a rainy day, I think Peg's that woman. I'll ask

Peg. If she refuse, I have no less than I have.'

David went that very evening, and opened his mind to Peg Ketchen. 'Peg, I have taken it into my head to have a wife to keep me decent, sober, and respectable, and I'm going to make you the first offer.'

'Thank you, sir; I'm singularly obliged to you. Only you may save yourself the trouble of making such an offer to me; for of all characters, a confirmed drunkard is the one that I dread most. You are a Sabbath-breaker; I know that. You are a profane swearer; I know that also. From these I think I could wean you; but a habitual drunkard it is out of the power of woman or man to reclaim. Oh, I would not be buckled to such a man for the world! As lang as Will Dunlop, or Jamie Inglis, or John Cheap, needed a dram, your last penny would go for it.'

'It is ower true you say, Peg, my bonny woman. But ye ken I can work weel, an' charge fully as weel; an' gin ye were to take the management o' the *proceeds*, as the writers ca't, I think things wad do better. Therefore, take a walk into the country with me on Sunday.'

'Did ever only leevin' hear the like o' that! preserve us a' to do weel an' right; the man's a heathen, an', I declare, just rinnin' to the deil wi' his een open. Wad ye hae me to profane the Sabbath-day, gaun rakin' athwart the country wi' a chap like you? Heigh-wow! I wad be come to a low mete then! What wad the auld wives by sayin' to the lads an' I were to do that? I can tell you what they wad be sayin', "What think ye o' your bonny Peg Ketchen now? When she should hae been at the kirk, like a decent lass, serving her Maker, she has been awa' flirtin' the hale Sunday wi' a drunken profligate, wha bilkit his auld uncle, an' sang himsel' hame frae London wi' a tied-up leg, like a broken sailor." Ha, ha, Davie! I ken ye, lad.'

'Now, you are rather too hard on me, Peg; I am proffering you the greatest honour I have in my power to bestow.'

'The greatest dishonour, you mean.'

'You know I am as good a tradesman as is in Scotland.'

'The mair's the pity! And wha's the best drinker i' Scotland? For it will lie atween you an' John Henderson and Will Dunlop; for, as for Tam Stalker, he's no ance to be compared wi' you.'

'But, Peg, my woman—my dear, bonny woman—hear me speak, will you?'

'No, no, David, I winna hear ye speak; sae dinna try to lead me into a scrape, for I tell you again, as I tauld ye already, that of a' characters i' the warld a confirmed drunkard is the most dangerous that a virtuous young woman can be connectit wi'. Depend on it, the heat o' your throat will soon burn the claes aff your back; an' how soon wad it burn them off mine too!—for, ye ken, a woman's claes are muckle easier brunt than a man's. Sae, gang your ways to the change-house, an' tak a dram wi' Will Dunlop; ye'll be a great deal the better o't. An', hear ye, dinna come ony mair to deave me wi' your love, and your offers o' marriage; for, there's my hand, I sall never court or marry wi' you. I hae mair respect for mysel' than that comes to.'

Was not Peg a sensible girl? I think she was. I still think she must naturally have been a shrewd girl; but no living can calculate what a woman will do when a man comes in the question. There is a feeling of dependence and subordination about their guileless hearts, in reference to the other sex, that can be wound up to any thing, either evil or good. Peg was obliged to marry David, after all her virtuous resolutions. The very night of the wedding he got drunk; and poor Peg, seeing what she had brought herself to, looked in his face with the most pitiful expression, while his drunken cronies made game of him, and were endless in their jests on 'Benedict the married man.' Peg saw the scrape she had brought herself into, but retreat was impracticable: so she resolved to submit to her fate with patience and resignation, and to make the most of a bad bargain that she could.

And a bad bargain she has had of it, poor woman, apparently having lost all heart several years ago, and submitted, along with three children, to pine out life in want and wretchedness. The wedding booze increased David's thirst so materially, that it did not subside, night or day, for nearly a fortnight, until a kind remonstrance, mixed with many tears, from his young wife, made him resolve to turn over a new leaf. So away David went into the country, and cleaned all the people's clocks early in the morning before the owners rose, for fear of making confusion or disturbance in the house afterwards:—David was very attentive and obliging that way. Of course the clocks got nothing more than a little oil on the principal wheels; but the charge was always fair and reasonable, seldom exceeding five shillings. Then all the bells in each house required new cranks and new wires. They needed neither, but only a little oil and scrubbing up; but these were a source of considerable emolument. Then he gathered in all the watches of the country which were not going well, cleaned them all, and put in a great many nominal mainsprings, and really would have made a great deal of money, had it not been for the petty changehouses, not one of which he could go by; and when he met with a drouthy crony like Captain Palmer, neither of them would rise while they had a sixpence between them.

But the parish minister of the old burgh of Caverton, though accounted a very parsimonious gentleman himself, had a sincere regard for the welfare of his flock, temporal as well as spiritual; and in his annual visit he charged every one of them, that, when David did any work for them, they were to pay the wife, and not him. The greater part of them acquiesced; but Wattie Henderson refused, and said, 'O, poor soul, ye dinna ken what he has to thole! Ye ken about his drinkin', but ye ken little thing about his drouth.'

The shifts that David was now put to for whisky were often very degrading, but still rather amusing. One day he and Dunlop went in to Mr Mercer's inn, David saying, 'I must try to get credit for a Hawick gill or two here to-day, else we'll both perish.' They went in, and called for the whisky. Mercer asked David if he had the money to pay for it? David confessed that he had not, but said Mr Elliot of Dodhope was owing him three-and-sixpence, and as he was in the town that day, he would give him an order on him, if he was afraid of the money coming through his hands. Mr

Mercer said he would never desire a better creditor than Gideon, and gave them their three gills of whisky; but on going and presenting his order to Mr Elliot, he found that he had never, in his life, been owing David any thing which he had not paid before he left the house.

Another time he met the clergyman, and said to him, 'You have been a great deal of money out of my pouch, sir, wi' your grand moral advices. I think you owe me one-and-sixpence about yon bells—would it be convenient to pay me to-day? I have very much need of it.'

'And what are you going to do with it, David? I wish I were owing you ten times the sum; I should know whom to pay it to, for you have a wife and family that are worth looking after; but if you tell me the sterling truth of your necessity, perhaps I may pay you.'

'Why, the truth is, sir—look yonder: yonder is Will Dunlop and Jamie Inglis, standing wi' their backs against the wa', very drouthy like. I wad like to gie them something, poor chiels, to drink.'

'Now, David, as I am convinced you have told me the sterling truth, and as there is no virtue I value higher, there is your eighteen-pence, although I shall tax myself with the payment of it a second time to Peg.'

'God bless you, sir!—God bless you! and may you never want a glass of whisky when you are longing as much for it as I am.'

Another day he came up with Will Dunlop, and said, 'O man, what hae ye on ye? for I'm just spitting sixpences.'

'I have just eighteen-pence,' said Dunlop, 'which I got from my wife to buy a shoulder of mutton for our dinner; and as it is of her own winning, I dare not part with it, for then, you know, the family would want their dinner.'

'It is a hard case any way,' said David; 'but I think the hardest side of it is, for two men, dying of thirst, to lose that eighteen-pence. Give it to me, and I'll try to make a shift.'

Dunlop gave it to him, and David went away to Wattie Henderson, an honest, good-natured, simple man, and said that his wife had sent him 'for a shoulder of mutton for their dinner, and she has limited me to a sum, you see (showing him the money). If you have a shoulder that suits the price, I must have it.'

'We can easily manage that, David,' said he; 'for see, here is a good cleaver; I can either add or diminish.' He cut off a shoulder. 'It is too heavy for the money, David; it comes to two-and-four-pence.'

'I wad like to hae the shoulder keepit hale, sir, as I suspect my sister is to dine with us to-day. Will you just allow me to carry the mutton over to the foot of the wynd, and see if Peg be pleased to advance the rest of the price?'

'Certainly,' said Mr Henderson; 'I can trust your wife with any thing.'

David set straight off with the shoulder of mutton to Mrs Dunlop, who declared that she had never got such a good bargain in the flesh-market before; and the two friends enjoyed their three gills of whisky exceedingly. Mr Henderson, wondering that neither the mutton nor the money was returned, sent over a servant to inquire about the matter. Poor Peg had neither ordered nor received the shoulder of mutton; and all that she and her three children had to dine upon, was six potatoes.

'Poor fellow,' said Wattie, 'if I had kend he had been sae dry, I wad hae wat his whistle to him without ony cheatery.'

At length there came one very warm September, and the thirst that some men suffered was not to be borne. David felt that in a short time his body would actually break into chinks with sheer drought, and that some shift was positively required to keep body and soul together. Luckily, at that very time a Colonel Maxwell came to the house of John Fairgrieve, an honest, decent man, who had made a good deal of money by care and parsimony, and lived within two or three miles of Caverton. The colonel came with his dog, his double-barrelled gun, and livery servant, and bargained with John, at a prodigiously high board, for himself and servant. He said, as his liberty of shooting lay all around there, he did not care how much board he paid for a few weeks, only John was to be sure to get them the best in the country, both to eat and drink. He did so—laying in wine and spirits, beef and mutton; and the colonel and his servant lived at heck and manger, the one boozing away in the room, and the other in the kitchen, in both of which every one who entered was treated liberally. In the forenoons the colonel thundered among the partridges; but he never killed any, as he was generally drunk from morning to night, and from night to morning.

At length, John's daughter, Joan, a comely and sensible girl, began rather to smell a rat; and she says to her father one day, 'Father, dinna ye think this grand cornel o' your's is hardly sickan a polished gentlemanly man as ane wad expect-o' ane o' his rank?'

'I dinna ken, Joan; the man's weel eneuch if he wadna swear sae whiles, whilk I like unco ill. But there's ae thing that's ayont my comprehension: I wish he may be cannie; for dinna ye hear that our cock begins to craw every night about midnight, an' our hens to cackle as gin they war a' layin' eggs thegither an' the feint an egg's amang them a'?'

Joan could not repress a laugh; so she turned her back, and took a hearty one, saying, when she recovered her breath, 'I think baith master an' man are very uncivil and worthless chaps.'

'If either the ane or the ither hae been unceevil to you, my woman, just tell me sae. Say but the word, an' I'll——'

'Na, na, father; dinna get intil a passion for nae-thing. I'll take care o' *mysel'*, if ye can but take care o' *yoursel'*. It is that that I'm put till't about. Dinna ye think that for a' your outlay ye're unco lang o' fingerin' ony o' their siller?'

John gave a hitch up with his shoulder, as if something had been biting it, rubbed his elbow, and then said, 'The siller will answer us as weel when it comes a' in a slump thegither; for then, ye ken, we can pop it into the bank; whereas, if it were coming in every day, or even every week, we might be mootering it away, spending it on this thing an' the ither thing.'

'Yes, father; but, consider, if ye shouldna get it ava. Is nae the cornel's chaise an' horses standin' ower at the Blue Bell?'

'Ay, that they are, an' at ten shillings a-day, too. Gin the cornel warna a very rich man, could he afford to pay that sae lang, think ye?'

'Weel, father, take ye my advice. Gang away ower to Mr Mather, o' the Bell, an' just see what the carriage an' horses are like; for I wadna wonder if ye had to arreest them yet for your expenses. Mr Mather's a gayen auld-farrant chap, and, it is said, kens every man's character the first time he hears him speak. He'll tell you at aince what kind o'man your grand cornel is. And by a' means, father, tak a good look o' the carriage an' the horses, that ye may ken them again, like.'

John knew that his daughter Joan was a shrewd sensible lassie; so, without more expostulation, he put on his Sunday clothes, went away to the old burgh of Caverton, and called on Mr Mather. No! there were no carriage nor horses there belonging to a Colonel Maxwell, nor ever had been. This was rather astounding news to John; but what astounded him more was a twinkling blink from the wick of Mr Mather's wicked black eye, and an ominous shake of his head. 'Pray tell me this, John,' said Mr Mather: 'does this grand colonel of yours ever crow like a cock, or cackle like a laying hen?'

John's jaws fell down. 'It's verra extrordner how ye should hae chanced to speer that question at me, sir,' said he; 'for the truth is, that, sin' ever that man came to our house, our cock has begun a crawin' at midnight, an' a' our hens-a-cackling, as the hale o' them had been laying eggs, an' yet no an egg amang them a'.'

'Ah, John, ye may drink to your expenses and board-wages, then; for I heard of a certain gentleman being amissing out of this town for a while past; and I likewise heard that he had borrowed a hunting-jacket, a dog, and a gun, from John Henderson.'

John went away home in very great wrath, resolved, I believe, to throttle the colonel and his servant both; but they had been watching his motions that day; and never returned to his house more, neither to crow like cocks, cackle like hens, drink whisky, or pay for their board and lodging.

Tom Brown was very angry at David about this, and reproved him severely for taking in an honest industrious old man. 'But, dear, man, what could a body do?' said David. 'A man canna dee for thirst if there's ony thing to be had to drink either for love or money.'

'But you should have wrought for your drink yoursel', David.'

'Wrought for my drink? An' what at pray? A' the house bells were gaun janglin' on, like broken pots, in their usual way; there wasna even the mainspring of a watch wanting. And as for the clocks, they just went on, tick-for-tick, tick-for-tick, with the most tedious and provoking monotony. I couldna think of a man, in the whole country, who didna ken my face, but John; an' I kend he was as able to keep me a wee while as ony other body. An' what's the great matter? I'll clean his watch an' his clock to him as lang as he lives, an' never charge him ony thing, gin it be nae a new mainspring whiles, an' we'll maybe come nearly equal again.'

The last time I saw Peg Ketchen—what a change! From one of the sprightliest girls in the whole country, she is grown one of the most tawdry, miserable-looking objects. There is a hopeless dejection in her looks, which I never saw equalled; and I am afraid, that, sometimes when she has it in her power, she may take a glass herself, and even get a basting, for no man can calculate what a drunken man will do.

Now, though I have mixed two characters together in these genuine and true sketches, my reason for thus publishing them is to warn and charge every virtuous maiden, whatever she does, never to wed with a habitual drunkard. A virtuous woman may reclaim a husband from almost every vice but that; but that will grow upon him to his dying day; and if she outlive him, he will leave her a penniless and helpless widow. It is well known the veneration I have for the fair sex, and I leave them this charge as a legacy, lest I should not be able to address them again.

from Chambers' Edinburgh Journal
No. 72 (15 June 1833)

THE FIRST SERMON

Once, on a lovely day—it was in spring—
I went to hear a splendid young divine
Preach his first sermon. I had known the youth
In a society of far renown,
But liked him not, he held his head so high;
And ever and anon would sneer, and pooh!
And cast his head all to one side, as if
In perfect agony of low contempt
At everything he heard, however just.
Men like not this, and poets least of all.

Besides, there are some outward marks of men
One scarcely can approve. His hair was red,
Almost as red as German sealing-wax;
And then so curled—What illustrious curls!
'Twas like a tower of strength. Oh, what a head
For Combe or Dr Spurzheim to dissect,
After 'twas polled! His shoulders rather narrow,
And pointed like two pins. And then there was
A primming round the mouth, of odious cast,
Bespeaking the proud vacancy within.

Well, to the Old Greyfriars' Church I went,
And many more with me. The place was crowded.
In came the beadle—then our hero follow'd
With gown blown like a mainsail, flowing on
To right and left alternate; the sleek beaver,
Down by his thigh keeping responsive time.

Oh, such a sight of graceful dignity
Never astounded heart of youthful dame!
But I bethought me, what a messenger
From the world's pattern of humility!

　The psalm was read with beauteous energy,
And sung. Then pour'd the prayer from such a face
Of simpering seriousness—it was a quiz—
A mockery of all things deem'd divine.
Some men such faces may have seen among
The Methodists and Quakers—but I never.
The eyes were closely shut—one cheek turn'd up;
The mouth quite long and narrow like a seam,
Holding no fit proportion with the mouths
Which mankind gape with. Then the high curl'd hair
With quiver and with shake, announced supreme
The heart's sincere devotion: unto whom?
Ask not—it is unfair! Suppose to Heaven,
To the fair maids around the gallery
Or to the gorgeous idol, Self-conceit.
Glad was my heart at last to hear the word,
That often long'd-for and desired word,
Which men yearn for as for the dinner-bell,
And now was beauteously pronounced, AY-MAIN!

　Now for the sermon. O ye ruling Powers
Of poesy sublime, give me to sing
The splendours of that sermon! The bold *hem*;
The look sublime that beam'd with confidence;
The three wipes with the cambric handkerchief;

The strut—the bob—and the impressive thump
Upon the holy Book! No notes were there,
No, not a scrap—All was intuitive,
Pouring like water from a sacred fountain,
With current unexhausted. Now the lips
Protruded, and the eyebrows lower'd amain,
Like Kean's in dark Othello. The red hair
Shook like the wither'd juniper in wind.
'Twas grand—o'erpowering!—Such an exhibition
No pen of poet can delineate.

But now, Sir Bard, the sermon? Let us hear
Somewhat of this same grand and promised sermon—
Aha, there comes the rub! 'Twas made of *scraps*,
Sketches from *Nature*, from old Johnson some,
And some from Joseph Addison—John Logan—Blair—
William Shakspeare—Young's Night Thoughts—
    The Grave—
Gillespie on the Seasons—Even the plain
Bold energy of Andrew Thomson here
Was press'd into the jumble. Plan or system
In it was not—no gleam of mind or aim—
A thing of shreds and patches—yet the blare
Went on for fifteen minutes, haply more.
The *hems!* and *haws!* began to come more close;
Three at a time. The cambric handkerchief
Came greatly in request. The burly head
Gave over tossing. The fine cheek grew red—
Then pale—then blue—then to a heavy crimson.
The beauteous dames around the galleries

Began to look dismay'd; their rosy lips
Wide open'd; and their bosoms heaving so,
You might have ween'd a rolling sea within.
The gruff sagacious elders peered up,
With one eye shut right knowingly, as if
The light oppress'd it—but their features
Show'd restlessness and deep dissatisfaction.

   The preacher set him down—open'd the Bible,
Gave half a dozen *hems*; arose again,
Then half a dozen more—It would not do!
In every line his countenance bespoke
The loss of recollection; all within
Became a blank—a chaos of confusion,
Producing nought but agony of soul.
His long lip quiver'd, and his shaking hand
Of the trim beaver scarcely could make seizure,
When, stooping, floundering, plaiting at the knees,
He—made his exit. But how I admired
The Scottish audience! There was neither laugh
Nor titter; but a softn'd sorrow
Portray'd in every face. As for myself,
I laugh'd till I was sick; went home to dinner,
Drank the poor preacher's health, and laugh'd again.

   But otherwise it fared with him; for he
Went home to his own native kingdom—Fife,
Pass'd to his father's stable—seized a pair
Of strong plough-bridle reins, and hang'd himself.

And I have oft bethought me it were best,
Since that outrageous scene, for young beginners
To have a sermon, either of their own
Or other man's. If printed, or if written,
It makes small difference—but have it there
At a snug opening of the blessed book
Which any time will open there at will,
And save your credit. While the consciousness
That there it is, will nerve your better part,
And bear you through the ordeal with acclaim.

THE FORTUNE TELLER

*Maldie, a wanton shepherdess, is to have her palm read by
Nora. The identities of a clairvoyant's customers are supposed
to be unknown, but Nora has been warned of Maldie's
identity, and her reputation is only too well known . . .*

OMNES. Yes, yes; our fortunes! our fortunes!
Mine, wife—Good Nora, mine—
Mine first, if you please.
   (*They push their hands before one another.*)
GEMEL. Hold: let us try this mighty skill of hers.
Our hands are much alike—go we all in,
And one by one return, wrapt from her view;
The palms alone will be seen—I'll bet she gives
Good, rich, and loving husbands to some men,
And wives to women.
HUTCHON. 'Tis well conceived.
As my best days are bye, I will attend
And witness her mistakes.
OMNES. Aye, aye, Hutchon shall witness.
HUTCHON. (*Aside to* NORA.) Fear not, thou shalt
 know all,
And all of them; pray give it home to some.
(*Exeunt all but* NORA. HUTCHON *stops and makes
      signs, to which she assents.*)
NORA. (*Chaunts aloud.*) Moules, be nigh!
Be yare!—be sly!
Tickle the ear and itch the eye;
And O, the trembling heart-strings ply,
Till the little toiler torpid lie

In the sickening wave of mystery.
(*Re-enter MALDIE wrapped in gown and hood, led by*
HUTCHON, who makes signs to NORA.)
Ah, what a pretty palm!—How white it is,
And warm and moist!—not over hard with work.
Ah me! what's this I see!—O fie! O fie!
                    (*MALDIE pulls in her hand.*)
Nay, show it me—I will say nothing out
That is unmeet, but only in your ear.
Oh, aye! Here's something of a Sunday eve,
And of a braken bush, I see!—A ring!
                    (*She offers to pull away her hand.*)
A snood, a kerchief, garters fringed with gold!
And oaths of love!—I see well how it is!
A W and a B!—Who can it be?
I would give much to know who owns this hand.
The business rests not here—nor half—nor tenth:
One—Two—Three—Four! O love
Bestow not all thy bounty upon one!
(*She pulls away her hand and whispers HUTCHON aside.*)
HUTCHON. She bids me ask if all of these are husbands?
NORA. Would'st thou wish it truly?—lovers, lovers!
Fear not, poor chuck, there is a husband here;
A quiet man, I wot—Sad doings though!
But all's full close—It is a right fair fortune—
Let me see—Boys—Four—Girls—Gramercy!
HUTCHON. What? what?
NORA. Children—children—brats.
HUTCHON. All to one husband?
NORA. Oh! Ah! Must I tell all? Eh?

from All-Hallow-Eve

THE SUPERNATURAL

KILMENY

Bonny Kilmeny gaed up the glen;
But it wasna to meet Duneira's men,
Nor the rosy monk of the isle to see,
For Kilmeny was pure as pure could be.
It was only to hear the Yorlin sing,
And pu' the cress-flower round the spring;
The scarlett hypp and the hyndberrye,
And the nut that hung frae the hazel tree;
For Kilmeny was pure as pure could be.
But lang may her minny look o'er the wa',
And lang may she seek i' the greenwood shaw;
Lang the laird of Duneira blame,
And lang, lang gree or Kilmeny come hame!

When many lang day had come and fled,
When grief grew calm, and hope was dead,
When mess for Kilmeny's soul had been sung,
When the bedes-man had prayed, and the dead bell
    rung:
Late, late in a gloamin when all was still,
When the fringe was red on the westlin hill,
The wood was sere, the moon i' the wane,
The reek o' the cot hung o'er the plain,
Like a little wee cloud in the world its lane;
When the ingle lowed wi' an eiry leme,
Late, late in the gloamin Kilmeny came hame!

'Kilmeny, Kilmeny, where have you been?
Lang hae we sought baith holt and dean;
By linn, by ford, and greenwood tree,
Yet you are halesome and fair to see.
Where gat you that joup o' the lily sheen?
That bonny snood o' the birk sae green?
And these roses, the fairest that ever were seen?—
Kilmeny, Kilmeny, where have you been?'

Kilmeny looked up with a lovely grace,
But nae smile was seen on Kilmeny's face;
As still was her look, and as still was her ee,
As the stillness that lay on the emerant lea,
Or the mist that sleeps on a waveless sea.
For Kilmeny had been she ken'd not where,
And Kilmeny had seen what she could not declare;
Kilmeny had been where the cock never crew,
Where the rain never fell, and the wind never blew.
But it seemed as the harp of the sky had rung,
And the airs of heaven played round her tongue,
When she spake of the lovely forms she had seen,
And a land where sin had never been;
A land of love, and a land of light,
Withouten sun, or moon, or night;
Where the river swa'd a living stream,
And the light a pure and cloudless beam;
The land of vision it would seem,
A still, an everlasting dream.

In yon green wood there is a waik,
And in that waik there is a wene,
And in that wene there is a maike,

That neither has flesh, nor blood, nor bane;
And down in yon greenwood he walks his lane.

In that green wene Kilmeny lay,
Her bosom hap'd wi' flowerets gay;
But the air was soft and the silence deep,
And bonny Kilmeny fell sound asleep.
She kenned nae mair, nor opened her ee,
Till waked by the hymns of a far countrye.

She woke on a couch of the silk sae slim,
All striped wi' the bars of the rainbow's rim;
And lovely beings round were rife,
Who erst had travelled mortal life;
And aye they smiled, and 'gan to speer,
'What spirit has brought this mortal here?'

'Lang have I ranged the world wide,'
A meek and reverend fere replied;
'Baith night and day I have watched the fair,
Eident a thousand years and mair.
Yes, I have watched o'er ilk degree,
Wherever blooms femenitye;
And sinless virgin, free of stain
In mind and body, fand I nane.
Never, since the banquet of time,
Found I a virgin in her prime,
Till late this bonnie maiden I saw
As spotless as the morning snaw:
Full twenty years she has lived as free
As the spirits that sojourn in this countrye:
I have brought her away frae the snares of men,
That sin or death she never may ken.'

They clasped her waist and her hands sae fair,
They kissed her cheek, and they kemed her hair;
And round came many a blooming fere,
Saying, 'Bonny Kilmeny, ye're welcome here!
Women are freed of the littand scorn:—
O, blessed be the day Kilmeny was born!
Now shall the land of spirits see,
Now shall it ken what a woman may be!
Many lang year in sorrow and pain,
Many lang year through the world we've gane,
Commissioned to watch fair womankind,
For it's they who nurse the immortal mind.
We have watched their steps as the dawning shone,
And deep in the greenwood walks alone;
By lily bower and silken bed,
The viewless tears have o'er them shed;
Have soothed their ardent minds to sleep,
Or left the couch of love to weep.
We have seen! we have seen! but the time maun come,
And the angels will weep at the day of doom!

'O, would the fairest of mortal kind
Aye keep these holy truths in mind,
That kindred spirits their motions see,
Who watch their ways with anxious ee,
And grieve for the guilt of humanitye!
O, sweet to Heaven the maiden's prayer,
And the sigh that heaves a bosom sae fair!
And dear to Heaven the words of truth,
And the praise of virtue frae beauty's mouth!
And dear to the viewless forms of air,
The mind that kythes as the body fair!

'O, bonny Kilmeny! free frae stain,
If ever you seek the world again,
The world of sin, of sorrow, and fear,
O tell of the joys that are waiting here;
And tell of the signs you shall shortly see;
Of the times that are now, and the times that shall be.'

They lifted Kilmeny, they led her away,
And she walked in the light of a sunless day:
The sky was a dome of crystal bright,
The fountain of vision, and fountain of light:
The emerant fields were of dazzling glow,
And the flowers of everlasting blow.
Then deep in the stream her body they laid,
That her youth and beauty never might fade:
And they smiled on heaven, when they saw her lie
In the stream of life that wandered by.
And she heard a song, she heard it sung,
She kend not where; but sae sweetly it rung,
It fell on her ear like a dream of the morn:—
'O! blest by the day Kilmeny was born!
Now shall the land of the spirits see,
Now shall it ken what a woman may be!
The sun that shines on the world sae bright,
A borrowed gleid frae the fountain of light;
And the moon that sleeks the sky sae dun,
Like a gouden bow, or a beamless sun,
Shall wear away and be seen nae mair,
And the angels shall miss them travelling the air.
But lang, lang after baith night and day,
When the sun and the world have fled away;
When the sinner has gane to his waesome doom,
Kilmeny shall smile in eternal bloom!'

They bore her away, she wist not how,
For she felt not arm nor rest below;
But so swift they wained her through the light,
'Twas like the motion of sound or sight;
They seemed to split the gales of air,
And yet nor gale nor breeze was there.
Unnumbered groves below them grew;
They came, they past, and backward flew,
Like floods of blossoms gliding on,
A moment seen, in a moment gone.
O, never vales to mortal view
Appeared like those o'er which they flew!
That land to human spirits given,
The lowermost vales of the storied heaven;
From thence they can view the world below,
And heaven's blue gates with sapphires glow,
More glory yet unmeet to know.

They bore her far to a mountain green,
To see what mortal never had seen;
And they seated her high on a purple sward,
And bade her heed what she saw and heard;
And note the changes the spirits wrought,
For now she lived in the land of thought.
She looked, and she saw nor sun nor skies,
But a crystal dome of a thousand dyes;
She looked, and she saw nae land aright,
But an endless whirl of glory and light:
And radiant beings went and came
Far swifter than wind, or the linked flame.
She hid her een frae the dazzling view;
She looked again, and the scene was new.

She saw a sun on a summer sky,
And clouds of amber sailing by;
A lovely land beneath her lay,
And that land had lakes and mountains gray;
And that land had valleys and hoary piles,
And marled seas and a thousand isles.
Its fields were speckled, its forests green,
And its lakes were all of the dazzling sheen,
Like magic mirrors, where slumbering lay
The sun and the sky, and the cloudlet gray;
Which heaved and trembled, and gently swung,
On every shore they seemed to be hung:
For there they were seen on their downward plain
A thousand times, and a thousand again;
In winding lake, and placid firth.
Little peaceful heavens in the bosom of earth.

Kilmeny sighed and seemed to grieve,
For she found her heart to that land did cleave;
She saw the corn wave on the vale,
She saw the deer run down the dale;
She saw the plaid and the broad claymore,
And the brows that the badge of freedom bore;—
And she thought she had seen the land before.

She saw a lady sit on a throne,
The fairest that ever the sun shone on:
A lion licked her hand of milk,
And she held him in a leish of silk;
And a leifu' maiden stood at her knee,
With a silver wand and melting ee;
Her sovereign shield till love stole in,
And poisoned all the fount within.

   Then a gruff untoward bedes-man came,
And hundit the lion on his dame;
And the guardian maid wi' the dauntless ee,
She dropped a tear, and left her knee;
And she saw till the queen frae the lion fled,
Till the bonniest flower of the world lay dead;
A coffin was set on a distant plain,
And she saw the red blood fall like rain:
Then bonny Kilmeny's heart grew sair,
And she turned away, and could look nae mair.

   Then the gruff grim carle girned amain,
And they trampled him down, but he rose again;
And he baited the lion to deeds of weir,
Till he lapped the blood to the kingdom dear;
And weening his head was danger-preef,
When crowned with the rose and clover leaf,
He gowled at the carle, and chased him away
To feed wi' the deer on the mountain gray.
He gowled at the carle, and he pecked at Heaven,
But his mark was set, and his arles given.
Kilmeny a while her een withdrew;
She looked again, and the scene was new.

   She saw below her fair unfurled
One half of all the glowing world,
Where oceans rolled, and rivers ran,
To bound the aims of sinful man.
She saw a people, fierce and fell,
Burst frae their bounds like fiends of hell;
There lilies grew, and the eagle flew,
And she herked on her ravening crew,

Till the cities and towers were wrapt in a blaze,
And the thunder it roared o'er the lands and the seas.
The widows wailed, and the red blood ran,
And she threatened an end to the race of man:
She never lened, nor stood in awe,
Till caught by the lion's deadly paw.
Oh! then the eagle swinked for life,
And brainzelled up a mortal strife;
But flew she north, or flew she south,
She met wi' the gowl of the lion's mouth.

With a mooted wing and waefu' maen,
The eagle sought her eiry again;
But lang may she cower in her bloody nest,
And lang, lang sleek her wounded breast,
Before she sey another flight,
To play wi' the norland lion's might.

But to sing the sights Kilmeny saw,
So far surpassing nature's law,
The singer's voice wad sink away,
And the string of his harp wad cease to play.
But she saw till the sorrows of man were by,
And all was love and harmony;—
Till the stars of heaven fell calmly away,
Like the flakes of snaw on a winter day.

Then Kilmeny begged again to see
The friends she had left in her ain countrye,
To tell of the place where she had been,
And the glories that lay in the land unseen;
To warn the living maidens fair,

The loved of Heaven, the spirits' care,
That all whose minds unmeled remain
Shall bloom in beauty when time is gane.

   With distant music, soft and deep,
They lulled Kilmeny sound asleep;
And when she awakened, she lay her lane,
All happed with flowers in the greenwood wene.
When seven lang years had come and fled;
When grief was calm, and hope was dead;
When scarce was remembered Kilmeny's name,
Late, late in a gloamin Kilmeny came hame.
And O, her beauty was fair to see,
But still and steadfast was her ee!
Such beauty bard may never declare,
For there was no pride nor passion there;
And the soft desire of maiden's een
In that mild face could never be seen.
Her seymar was the lily flower,
And her cheek the moss-rose in the shower;
And her voice like the distant melodye,
That floats along the twilight sea.
But she loved to raike the lanely glen,
And keep afar frae the haunts of men;
Her holy hymns unheard to sing,
To suck the flowers and drink the spring.
But wherever her peaceful form appeared,
The wild beasts of the hill were cheered;
The wolf played blythely round the field,
The lordly byson lowed and kneeled;
The dun deer wooed with manner bland,
And cowered aneath her lily hand.

And when at eve the woodlands rung,
When hymns of other worlds she sung
In ecstacy of sweet devotion,
O, then the glen was all in motion!
The wild beasts of the forest came,
Broke from their boughts and faulds the tame,
And goved around, charmed and amazed;
Even the dull cattle crooned and gazed,
And murmured and looked with anxious pain
For something the mystery to explain.
The buzzard came with the throstle-cock;
The corby left her houf in the rock;
The blackbird alang wi' the eagle flew;
The hind came tripping o'er the dew;
The wolf and the kid their raike began,
And the tod, and the lamb, and the leveret ran;
The hawk and the hern attour them hung,
And the merl and the mavis forhooyed their young;
And all in peaceful ring were hurled:—
It was like an eve in a sinless world!

When a month and a day had come and gane,
Kilmeny sought the greenwood wene;
There laid her down on the leaves sae green,
And Kilmeny on earth was never mair seen.
But O, the words that fell from her mouth,
Were words of wonder and words of truth!
But all the land were in fear and dread,
For they kendna whether she was living or dead.
It wasna her hame and she couldna remain;
She left this world of sorrow and pain,
And returned to the land of thought again.

WHAT IS DEATH?

GEORGE. Who is this fellow Death that kills so many people brother Tom?

TOM. I don't know who he is. I never saw him, but I have seen his picture. He is a fellow without either skin or flesh on his bones a mere skeleton. A very ugly fellow indeed, with a long scythe over his shoulder with which he cuts down and kills all the men and women of the whole world when ever he can get at them.

GEORGE. He must be a giant; and a very bad wicked fellow too. I do not understand him. Did not God make all the men women and children in the world brother?

TOM. Yes—God made them all.

GEORGE. Then what has Death ado to kill them? If Gorge were God him would fight him.

TOM. I have often thought that if I were a big strong man I would like to fight him and thrash him and smash him dead; for you know he killed our dear good sister George, our kind little Laura.

GEORGE. So he did. And you are to let me help you to kill him Tom for I like him very bad. Did God make Death too brother?

TOM. I don't know. I do not think God would make him; for I think he would not make so many strong men, and lovely women, and good pretty children, and then make an ugly monster of a rascal to kill them all again. I rather think he is a ghost.

GEORGE. Hold your peace and don't say so brother else you will make me frightened for him, and that is what I cannot bear to think of; for if I live I intend to meet him face to face, and dare him, and smite him down with a sharp sword, or a very long spear on the end of a pole. But if he be a ghost how can I do that?

TOM. I suspect he is the ghost of some wicked cruel king, or perhaps that of Cain the first shedder of human blood. But I really don't know who or what he is. However yonder comes Cousin Mary to take us home to school we will ask her. Can you tell us cousin who death is, or who made him? For George and I want to fight him for killing our poor sister.

MARY. You are brave little boys, of manly and generous natures, but you speak you not know what. And you must learn to speak of death with more awe and reverence.

BOTH. Who is he Mary? Who is he?

MARY. He is the Sovereign of the Grave, and sends forth his invisible emissaries in thousands over the whole face of the earth to cut off mankind in every stage of their life. Yet no man needs to be afraid of Death, for there is one who is his master, and he can only take such as God hath appointed him.

GEORGE. Did God make him at first Cousin Mary?

MARY. No my dear boy. Men brought death upon themselves. God made man at first pure and upright; but man brought sin into the world, and Death came with it; and so Death still passes upon all men for all have sinned.

TOM. Who is it then that has mastered him?

MARY. It is Jesus Christ the Son of the living God; he

who came from heaven and redeemed us with his own blood. These our bodies that grow up here like flowers to perish and decay are all subject to death, and the grave. But Jesus Christ by the sacrifice of himself conquered both, and we shall all rise again in the vigour of youth and beauty, go to a better and more glorious country, and continue to improve in knowledge righteousness and holiness to all the ages of Eternity.

GEORGE. Will we improve in strength too cousin Mary?

MARY. Yes both in strength and beauty.

GEORGE. Then poor little George likes no body so well as Jesus Christ. He always loved him, but he felt that he loved his father and mother better. But they have not died for him and now George loves his Saviour better than all the world.

MARY. May the blessing of heaven rest upon my two little good cousins. And now come away home with me to school.

from 'Dramas of Infancy'

A TALE OF THE MARTYRS

Red Tam Harkness came into the farm-house of Garrick, in the parish of Closeburn, one day, and began to look about for some place to hide in, when the goodwife, whose name was Jane Kilpatrick, said to him in great alarm, 'What's the matter, what's the matter, Tam Harkness?'

'Hide me, or else I'm a dead man: that's the present matter, goodwife,' said he. 'But yet, when I have time, if ever I hae mair time, I have heavy news for you. For Christ's sake, hide me, Jane, for the killers are hard at hand.'

Jane Kilpatrick sprung to her feet but she was quite benumbed and powerless. She ran to one press, and opened it, and then to another; there was not room to stuff a clog into either of them. She looked into a bed; there was no shelter there, and her knees began to plait under her weight with terror. The voices of the troopers were by this time heard fast approaching, and Harkness had no other shift, but in one moment to conceal himself behind the outer door, which stood open, yet the place where he stood was quite dark. He heard one of them say to another, 'I fear the scoundrel is not here after all. Guard the outhouses.'

On that three or four of the troopers rushed by him, and began to search the house and examine the inmates. Harkness that moment slid out without being observed, and tried to escape up a narrow glen called Kinrivvah, immediately behind the house; but unluckily two troopers, who had been in another chase, there met him in the face. When he perceived them he turned and ran to the eastward; on which they both fired, which raised the alarm, and instantly the whole pack were after him. It was afterwards conjectured that one of the shots had wounded him, for, though he, with others, had been nearly surrounded that morning, and twice waylaid, he had quite outrun the soldiers; but now it was observed that some of them began to gain ground on him, and they still continued firing, till at length he fell in a kind of slough east from the farm-house of Locherben, where they came up to him, and ran him through with their bayonets. The spot is called Red Tam's Gutter to this day.

Jane Kilpatrick was one of the first who went to his mangled corpse,—a woful sight, lying in the slough, and sore did she lament the loss of that poor and honest man. But there was more; she came to his corpse by a sort of yearning impatience to learn what was the woful news he had to communicate to her. But, alas, the intelligence was lost, and the man to whose bosom alone it had haply been confided was no more; yet Jane could scarcely prevail on herself to have any fears for her own husband, for she knew him to be in perfectly safe hiding in Glen-Gorar; still Tam's last words hung heavy on her mind. They were both suspected to have been at the harmless rising at Enterkin, for the relief of a favourite minister, which was effected; and that was the extent of their crime. And though it was only suspicion, four men were shot on the hills that morning, without trial or examination, and their bodies forbidden Christian burial.

One of these four was John Weir of Garrick, the husband of Jane Kilpatrick, a man of great worth and honour, and universally respected. He had left his hiding-place in order to carry some intelligence to his friends, and to pray with them, but was entrapped among them and slain. Still there was no intelligence brought to his family, save the single expression that fell from the lips of Thomas Harkness in a moment of distraction. Nevertheless Jane could not rest, but set out all the way to her sister's house in Glen-Gorar, in Crawford-muir, and arrived there at eleven o'clock on a Sabbath evening. The family being at prayers when she went, and the house dark, she stood still behind the hallan, and all the time was convinced that the voice of the man that prayed was the voice of her husband, John Weir. All the time that fervent prayer lasted the tears of joy ran from her eyes, and her heart beat with gratitude to her Maker as she drank into her soul every sentence of the petitions and thanksgiving. Accordingly, when worship was ended, and the candle lighted, she went forward with a light heart and joyful countenance, her sister embraced her, though manifestly embarrassed and troubled at seeing her there at such a time. From her she flew to embrace her husband, but he stood like a statue, and did not meet her embrace. She gazed at him—she grew pale, and, sitting down, she covered her face with her apron. This man was one of her husband's brothers, likewise in hiding, whom she had never before seen, but the tones of his voice, and even the devotional expressions that he used, were so like her husband's, that she mistook them for his.

All was now grief and consternation, for John Weir had not been seen or heard of since Wednesday evening, when he had gone to warn his friends of some impending danger; but they all tried to comfort each other as well as they could, and, in particular, by saying they were all in the Lord's hand, and it behoved him to do with them as seemed to him good, with many other expressions of piety and submission. But the next morning, when the two sisters were about to part, the one says to the other, 'Jane, I cannot help telling you a strange confused dream that I had just afore ye wakened me. Ye ken I pit nae faith in dreams, and I dinna want you to regard it; but it is as good for friends to tell them to ane anither, and then, if ought turn out like it in the course o' providence, it may bring it to baith their minds that their spirits had been conversing with God.'

'Na, na, Aggie, I want nane o' your confused dreams. I hae other things to think o', and mony's the time an' oft ye hae deaved me wi' them, an' sometimes made me angry.'

'I never bade ye believe them, Jeanie, but I likit ay to tell them to you, and this I daresay rase out o' our conversation yestreen. But I thought I was away, ye see, I dinna ken where I was; and I was fear'd and confused, thinking I had lost my way. And then I came to an auld man, an' he says to me, "Is it the road to heaven that you are seeking, Aggie?" An' I said, "Aye," for I didna like to deny't.

"Then I'll tell you where ye maun gang," said he, "ye

maun gang up by the head of yon dark, mossy cleuch, an' you will find ane there that will show you the road to heaven;" and I said, "Aye," for I didna like to refuse, although it was an uncouth-looking road, and ane that I didna like to gang. But when I gangs to the cleuch head, wha does I see sitting there but your ain goodman, John Weir, and I thought I never saw him look sae weel; and when I gaed close up to him, there I sees another John Weir, lying strippit to the sark, an' a' beddit in blood. He was cauld dead, and his head turned to the ae side; and when I saw siccan a sight, I was terrified, an' held wide off him. But I gangs up to the living John Weir, and says to him, "Gudeman, how's this?"

"Dinna ye see how it is, sister Aggie?" says he, "I'm just set to herd this poor man that's lying here."

"Then I think ye'll no' hae a sair post, John," says I, "for he disna look as he wad rin far away." It was a very unreverend speak o' me, sister, but these were the words that I thought I said; an' as it is but a dream, ye ken ye needna heed it.

"Alas, poor Aggie!" says he, "ye are still in the gall o' bitterness yet. Look o'er your right shoulder, an' you will see what I hae to do." An sae I looks o'er my right shoulder, an' there I sees a haill drove o' foxes an' wulcats, an' fumarts an' martins, an' corbey craws, an' a hunder vile beasts, a' stannin' round wi' glarin een, eager to be at the corpse o' the dead John Weir; an' then I was terribly astoundit, an' I says to him, "Goodman, how's this?"

"I am commissioned to keep these awa," says he. "Do you think these een that are yet to open in the light o' heaven, and that tongue that has to syllable the praises of a Redeemer far within yon sky, should be left to become the prey o' siccan vermin as these!"

"Will it make sae verra muckle difference, John Weir," says I, "whether the carcass is eaten up by these or by the worms?"

"Ah, Aggie, Aggie! worms are worms; but ye little wat what these are," says he. "But John Weir has warred with them a' his life, an' that to some purpose, and they maunna get the advantage o' him now."

"But which is the right John Weir?" says I, "for here is ane lying stiff and lappered in his blood, and another in health and strength and sound mind."

"I am the right John Weir," says he. "Did ye ever think the goodman o' Garrick could die? Na, na, Aggie; Clavers can only kill the body, an' that's but the poorest part of the man. But where are you gaun this wild gate?"

"I was directed this way on my road to heaven," says I.

"Ay, an' ye were directed right then," says he. "For this is the direct path to heaven, and there is no other."

"That is very extraordinary," says I. "And, pray, what is the name of this place, that I may direct my sister Jane, your wife, and all my friends, by the same way?"

"This is Faith's Hope," says he.'

But behold, at the mention of this place, Jane Kilpatrck of Garrick rose slowly up to her feet and held up both her hands. 'Hold, hold, sister Aggie,' cried she, 'you have told enough. Was it in the head of

Faith's Hope that you saw this vision of my dead husband?'

'Yes; but at the same time I saw your husband alive.'

'Then I fear your dream has a double meaning,' said she. 'For though it appears like a religious allegory, you do not know that there really is such a place, and that not very far from our house. I have often laughed at your dreams, sister, but this one hurries me from you to-day with a heavy and a trembling heart.'

Jane left Glen-Gorar by the break of day, and took her way through the wild ranges of Crawford-muir, straight for the head of Faith's Hope. She had some bread in her lap, and a little bible that she always carried with her, and without one to assist or comfort her, she went in search of her lost husband. Before she reached the head of of that wild glen, the day was far spent, and the sun wearing down. The valley of the Nith lay spread far below her, in all its beauty, but around her there was nothing but darkness, dread, and desolation. The mist hovered on the hills, and on the skirts of the mist the ravens sailed about in circles, croaking furiously, which had a most ominous effect on the heart of poor Jane. As she advanced farther up, she perceived a fox and an eagle sitting over against each other, watching something which yet they seemed terrified to approach; and right between them in a little green hollow, surrounded by black haggs, she found the corpse of her husband in the same manner as described by her sister. He was stripped of his coat and vest, which it was thought, he had thrown from him when flying from the soldiers, to enable him to effect his escape. He was shot through the heart with two bullets, but nothing relating to his death was ever known, whether he died praying, or was shot as he fled; but there was he found lying, bathed in his blood, in the wilderness, and none of the wild beasts of the forest had dared to touch his lifeless form.

The bitterness of death was now past with poor Jane. Her staff and shield was taken from her right hand, and laid low in death by the violence of wicked men. True, she had still a home to go to, although that home was robbed and spoiled; but she found that without *him* it was no home, and that where his beloved form reposed, that was the home of her rest. She washed all his wounds, and the stains of blood from his body, tied her napkin round his face, covered him with her apron, and sat down and watched beside him all the live-long night, praying to the Almighty, and singing hymns and spiritual songs alternately. The next day she warned her friends and neighbours, who went with her on the following night, and buried him privately in the north-west corner of the churchyard of Morton. The following verses are merely some of her own words versified, as she was sitting by his corpse in the wild glen, or rather the thoughts that she described as having passed through her heart.

> I canna greet for thee, my John Weir,
>   oh, I canna greet for thee:
> For the hand o Heaven lies heavy here,
>   and this sair wird I maun dree.
> They harried us first o cow and ewe,
>   with curses and cruelty,

And now they hae shed thy dear life blood,
    an what's to become o me?
I am left a helpless widow here;
    oh, what's to become of me?

I hae born thee braw young sons, John Weir,
    and nursed them upon my knee;
But two are fled to their father's hame
    frae the evils awaiting thee.
Their little green graves lie side by side
    like twins in fond ally,
But in beside thy children dear
    thy dust maun never lie—
Like an outcast o the earth John Weir
    in the moorland thou maun lie.

But though thou lie at the back o the dyke,
    or in hagg o the mountain lee,
Wherever thy loved dust remains
    is sacred ground to me.
And there I will watch, and there I will pray,
    for tears I now hae nane,
For the injuries done by wicked men
    have speared my simple brain.
Even over thy pale corpse John Weir,
    I try to weep in vain.

But soon shall our oppressors' sway
   in desolation lie,
Like autumn flowers it shall decay
   and in its foulness die.
The tyrant's name, the tyrant's reign,
   whose rule hath never thriven,
The blood of saints hath blotted out
   both from the earth and Heaven—
For this dear blood of thine, John Weir
   can never be forgiven.

THE WITCH O' FIFE

Hurray, hurray, the jade's away,
　　Like a rocket of air with her bandalet!
I'm up in the air on my bonnie gray mare,
　　But I see her yet, I see her yet.
I'll ring the skirts o' the gowden wain
　　Wi' curb an' bit, wi' curb an' bit:
An' catch the Bear by the frozen mane—
　　An' I see her yet, I see her yet.

Away, away, o'er mountain an' main,
　　To sing at the morning's rosy yett;
An' water my mare at its fountain clear—
　　But I see her yet, I see her yet.
Away, thou bonnie witch o' Fife,
　　On foam of the air to heave an' flit,
An' little reck thou of a poet's life,
　　For he sees thee yet, he sees thee yet!

THE WITCHES OF TRAQUAIR

There was once a young man, a native of Traquair, in the county of Peebles, whose name was Colin Hyslop, and who suffered more by witchcraft, and the intervention of supernatural beings, than any man I ever heard of. But the tale is a very old one, and sorry am I to say that I cannot vouch for the truth of it, which I have hitherto, for the most part, been accustomed to do, and which I feel greatly disposed to do at all times, provided the tale bears the marks of authenticity impressed on the leading events, whether I know of a verity that every individual incident related *did* happen or not.

Traquair was a terrible place then! There was a witch almost in every hamlet, and a warlock here and there besides. There were no fewer than twelve witches in one straggling hamlet, called Taniel-Burn, and five in Kirk-Row. What a desperate place Traquair had been in those days! But there is no person who is so apt to overshoot his mark as the Devil. He must be a great fool in the main; for, with all his high-flying and democratic principles, he often runs himself into the most confounded blunders that ever the leader of an opposition got in to the midst of. Throughout all the annals of the human race, it is manifest, that whenever he was aiming to do the most evil, he was uniformly bringing about the most good;

and it seems to have been so in the age to which my tale refers.

The truth is, that Popery was then on its last legs, and the Devil, finding it (as then exercised) a very convenient and profitable sort of religion, exerted himself beyond measure to give its motley hues a little more variety; and the plan of making witches and warlocks, and of holding nocturnal revels with them, where every sort of devilry was exercised, was at that time with him a favourite measure. It was also favourably received by the meaner sort of the populace. Witches gloried in their power, and warlocks in their foreknowledge of events, and the energies of their master. Women, beyond a certain age, when the pleasures and hopes of youth delighted no more, flew to it as an excitement of a higher and more terrible nature; and men, whose tempers had been soured by disappointment and ill usage, betook themselves to the Prince of the Power of the Air, enlisting under his banner, in hopes of obtaining revenge on their oppressors. However extravagant this may appear, there is no doubt of the fact, that, in those days, the hopes of attaining some energies beyond the reach of mere human capability, inflamed the ignorant and wicked to attempts and acts of the most diabolical nature; for hundreds acknowledged their principles, and gloried in them, before the tribunals that adjudged them to the stake.

'I am now fairly under the power of witchcraft,' said Colin Hyslop, as he sat on the side of the Feathen Hill, with his plaid drawn over his head, the tears running down his brown manly cheek, and a paper marked with uncouth lines and figures in his hand,—'I am now fairly under the power of witchcraft, and must submit to my fate; I am entangled, enchained, enslaved; and the fault is all my own, for I have committed that degree of sin which my sainted and dying father assured me would subject me to the snares of my hellish neighbours and sworn adversaries. My pickle sheep have a' been bewitched, and a great part o' them have died dancing hornpipes an' French curtillions. I have been changed, and ower again changed, into shapes and forms that I darena think of, far less name; and a' through account of my ain sin. Hech! but it is a queer thing that sin! It has sae mony inroads to the heart, and outlets by the senses, that we seem to live and breathe in it. And I canna trow that the Deil is the wyte of a' our sins neither. Na, na; black as he is, he canna be the cause and the mover of a' our transgressions, for I find them often engendering and breeding in my heart as fast as maggots on tainted carrion, and then it is out o' the power of man to keep them down. My father tauld me, that if I aince let the Deil get his little finger into *ane* o' my transactions, he wad soon hae his haill hand into them a'. Now, I hae found it in effect, but not in belief; for, from a' that I can borrow frae Rob Kirkwood, the warlock, and my aunty Nans, the wickedest witch in Christendye, the Deil appears to me to be a gayan obliging chap. That he is wayward and fond o' sin, I hae nae doubt; but in that he has mony neighbours. And then his great power over the senses and conditions of men, over the winds, the waters, and the element of flame, is to me incomprehensible, and shows him to be rather a sort of vicegerent over the outskirts and unruly parts of nature, than an opponent to its lawful lord.—What then shall I do with this?' looking at the scroll; 'shall I subscribe to the conditions, and enlist under his banner, or shall I not? O love, love! were it not for thee, all the torments that old Mahoun and his followers could inflict should not induce me to quit the plain path of Christianity. But that disdainful, cruel, and lovely Barbara! I must and will have her, though my repentance should be without measure and without end. So then it is settled! Here I will draw blood from my arm—blot out the sign of the cross with it, and form that of the crescent, and these other things, the meaning of which I do not know.—Hilloa! What's that? Two beautiful deers, as I am a sinner, and one of them lame. What a prey for poor ruined Colin! and fairly-off the royal bounds too. Now for it, Bawty, my fine dog! now for a clean chase! A' the links o' the Feathen-wood winna hide them from your infallible nose, billy Bawty. Halloo! off you go, sir! and now for the bow and the broad arrow at the head slap!—What! ye winna hunt a foot-length after them, will ye no? Then, Bawty, there's some mair mischief in the wind for me! I see what your frighted looks tell me. That they dinna leave the scent of other deers on their track, but ane that terrifies you, and makes your blood creep. It is hardly possible, ane wad think, that witches could assume the shape of these bonny harmless creatures; but their power has come to sic a height hereabouts, that nae man alive can tell what they can do. There's my aunty Nans has already turned me into a goat, then to a gander, and last of all into a three-legged stool.

'I am a ruined man, Bawty! your master is a ruined man, and a lost man, that's far waur. He has sold himself for love to one beautiful creature, the comeliest of all the human race. And yet that beautiful creature must be a witch, else how could a' the witches o' Traquair gie me possession o' her?

'Let me consider and calculate. Now, suppose they are deceiving me—for that's their character; and suppose they can never put me in possession of her, then I hae brought myself into a fine habble. How terrible a thought this is! Let me see; is all over? Is this scroll signed and sealed; and am I wholly given up to this unknown and untried destiny?' (Opens his scroll with trembling agitation, and looks over it.) 'No, thanks to the Lord of our universe, I am yet a Christian. The cross stands uncancelled, and there is neither sign nor superscription in my blood. How did this happen? I had the blood drawn—the pen filled—and the scroll laid out. Let me consider what it was that prevented me? The deers? It was, indeed, the two comely deers. What a strange intervention this is! Ah! these were no witches! but some good angels, or happy fays, or guardian spirits of the wild, sent to snatch an abused youth from destruction. Now, thanks be to Heaven, though poor and reduced to the last extremity, I am yet a free man, and in my Maker's hand. My resolution is changed—my promise is broken, and here I give this mystic scroll to the winds of the glen.

'Alas, alas! to what a state sin has reduced me! Now shall I be tortured by night, and persecuted by day;

changed into monstrous shapes, torn by cats, pricked by invisible bodkins, my heart racked by insufferable pangs of love, until I either lose my reason, and yield to the dreadful conditions held out to me, or lose all hope of earthly happiness, and yield up my life. Oh, that I were as free of sin as that day my father gave me his last blessing! then might I withstand all their charms and enchantments. But that I will never be. So as I have brewed so must I drink. These were his last words to me, which I may weel remember:—"You will have many enemies of your soul to contend with, my son; for your nearest relations are in compact with the devil; and as they have hated and persecuted me, so will they hate and persecute you; and it will only be by repeating your prayers evening and morning, and keeping a conscience void of all offence towards God and towards man, that you can hope to escape the snares that will be laid for you. But the good angels from the presence of the Almighty will, perhaps, guard my poor orphan boy, and protect him from the counsels of the wicked."

'Now, in the first place, I have never prayed at all; and, in the second place, I have sinned so much, that I have long ago subjected myself to their snares, and given myself up for lost. What will become of me? flight is in vain, for they can fly through the air, and follow me to Flanders. And then, Barbara,—O that lovely and bewitching creature! in leaving her I would leave life and saul behind!'

After this long and troubled soliloquy, poor Colin burst into tears, and wished himself a dove, or a sparrow-hawk, or an eagle, to fly away and be seen no more; but, in either case, to have bonny Barbara for his mate. At this instant Bawty began to cock up his ears, and turn his head first to the one side and then to the other; and, on Colin looking up, he beheld two hares cowering away from a bush behind him. There was nothing that Colin was so fond of as a hunt. He sprung up, pursued the hares, and shouted, Halloo, halloo! to Bawty. No, Bawty would not pursue them a foot, but whenever he came to the place where he had seen them, and put his nose to the ground, ran back, hanging his tail, and uttering short barks, as he was wont to do when attacked by witches in the night. Colin's hair rose up on his head, for he instantly suspected that the two hares were Robin Kirkwood and his aunt Nans, watching his motions, and the fulfilment of his promise to them. Colin was horrified, and knew not what to do. He did not try to pray, for he could not; but he wished, in his heart, that his father's dying-prayer for him had been heard.

He rose, and hastened away in the direction contrary to that the hares had taken, as may well be supposed; and as he jogged along, in melancholy mood, he was aware of two damsels, who approached him slowly and respectfully. They were clothed in white, with garlands on their heads; and, on their near approach, Colin perceived that the one of them was lame, and the other supported her by the hand. The two comely hinds that had come upon him so suddenly and unexpectedly, and had prevented him, at the very decisive moment, from selling his salvation for sensual enjoyment, instantly came over Colin's awakened recollection, and he was struck with indescribable awe. Bawty was affected somewhat in the same manner with his master. He did not manifest the same sort of dismay as when attacked by witches and warlocks, but crept close to the ground, and turning his face half away from the radiant objects, uttered a sort of stifled murmur, as if moved both by respect and fear. Colin perceived, from these infallible symptoms, that the beings with whom he was now coming in contact were not the subjects of the Power of Darkness.

Colin, throwing his plaid over his shoulder in the true shepherd-style, took his staff below his left arm, so that his right hand might be at liberty to lift his bonnet when the fair damsels accosted him, and, not choosing to run straight on them, face to face, he paused at a respectful distance, straight in their path. When they came within a few paces of him, they turned gently from the path, as if to pass him on the left side, but all the while kept their bright eyes fixed on him, and whispered to each other. Colin was grieved that so much comeliness should pass without saluting him, and kept his regretful eyes steadily on them. At length they paused, and one of them called, in a sweet but solemn voice, 'Ah, Colin Hyslop, Colin Hyslop! you are on the braid way for destruction.'

'How do ye ken that, madam?' returned Colin. 'Do you ca' the road up the Kirk-rigg the braid way to destruction?'

'Ay, up the rigg or down the rigg, cross the rigg or round the rigg, all is the same for you, Colin. You are a lost man; and it is a great pity. One single step farther on the path you are now treading, and all is over.'

'What wad ye hae me to do, sweet madam? Wad ye hae me to stand still an' starve here on the crown o' the Kirk-rigg?'

'Better starve in a dungeon than take the steps you are about to take. You were at a witch and warlock meeting yestreen.'

'It looks like as gin you had been there too, madam, that you ken sae weel.'

'Yes, I *was* there, but under concealment, and not for the purpose of making any such vows and promises as you made. O wretched Colin Hyslop, what is to become of you!'

'I did naething, madam, but what I couldna help; and my heart is sair for it the day.'

'Can you lay your heart on that heart and swear to it and say so?'

'Yes, I can, dear madam, and swear to it too.'

'Then follow us down to this little green knowe, and recount to us the circumstances of your life, and I will inform you of a secret I heard yestreen.'

'Aha, madam, but yon is a fairy ring, and I hae gotten sae mony cheats wi' changelings, that I hae muckle need to be on my guard. However, things can hardly be waur wi' me. Lead on, and I shall e'en follow.'

The two female figures walked before him to a fairy knowe, on the top of the Feathen-hill, and sat down, with their faces towards him, till he recounted the incidents of his life, which were of a horrible kind, and not to be set down. The outline was thus:—His father was a sincere adherent of the Reformers, and a good Christian; but poor Colin was born at Taniel-Burn, in the midst of Papists and witches; and the nearest relation he had, a maternal aunt, was the leading witch of the whole neighbourhood. Consequently, Colin was nurtured in sin, and injured to iniquity, until all the kindly and humane principles of his nature were erased, or so much distorted, as to appear like their very opposites; and when this was accomplished, his wicked aunt and her associate hags, judging him fairly gained, without the pale of redemption, began to exercise cantrips, the most comical, and, at the same time, the most refined in cruelty, at his expense; and at length, on being assured of every earthly enjoyment, he engaged to join their hellish community, only craving three days to study their mysteries, bleed himself, and, with the blood extracted from his veins, extinguish the sign of the cross, thereby renouncing his hope in mercy, and likewise make some hierogly-phics of strange shapes and mysterious efficacy, and finally subscribe his name to the whole.

When the relation was finished, one of the lovely auditors said,— 'You are a wicked and abandoned person, Colin Hyslop. But you were reared up in iniquity, and know no better; and the mercy of Heaven is most readily extended to such. You have, besides, some good points in your character still; for you have told us the truth, however much to your own disadvantage.'

'Aha, madam! How do you ken sae weel that I hae been telling you a' the truth?'

'I know all concerning you better than you do yourself. There is little, very little, of a redeeming nature in your own history; but you had an upright and devout father, and the seed of the just may not perish for ever. I have been young, and now am old, yet have I never seen the good man forsaken, nor his children cast out as vagabonds in the land of their fathers.'

'Ah, na, na, madam! ye canna be auld. It is impossible! But goodness kens! there are sad changelings now-a-days. I hae seen an auld wrinkled wife blooming o'er night like a cherub.'

'Colin, you are a fool! And folly in youth leads to misery in old age. But I am your friend, and you have not another on earth this night but myself and sister here, and one more. Pray, will you keep this little vial, and drink it for my sake?'

'Will it no' change me, madam?'

'Yes, it will.'

'Then I thank you; but keep it. I have had enow of these kind o' drinks in my life.'

'But suppose it change you for the better? Suppose it change you to a new creature?'

'Weel, suppose it should, what will the creature be? Tell me that first. Will it no be a fox, nor a gainder, nor a bearded gait, nor a three-fitted stool?'

'Ah, Colin, Colin!' exclaimed she, smiling through tears, 'your own wickedness and unbelief gave the agents of perdition power over you. It is that power which I wish to counteract. But I will tell you nothing more. If you will not take this little vial, and drink it, for my sake; why, then, leave it, and follow on your course.'

'O, dear madam! ye ken little thing about me. I was only joking wi' you for the sake o' hearing your sweet answers. For were that bit glass fu' o' rank poison, and were it to turn me intil a taed or worm, I wad drink it aff at your behest. I hae been sae little accustomed to hear aught serious or friendly, that my very heart clings to to you as it wad do to an angel coming down frae heaven to save me. Ay, and ye said something kind and respectfu' about my auld father too. That's what I hae been as little used to. Ah, but he was a douce man! Wasna he, mem? Drink that bit bottle o' liquor for your sake! Od, I wish it were fu' to the brim, and that's no what it is by twa thirds.'

'Ay, but it has this property, Colin, that drinking will never exhaust it; and the langer you drink it, the sweeter it will become.'

'Sae you sae? Then here's till ye. We'll see whether drinking winna exhaust it or no.'

Colin set the vial to his lips, with intent of draining it; but the first portion that he swallowed made him change his countenance, and shudder from head to heel.

'Ah! sweeter did you say, madam? by the faith of my heart, it has muckle need; for sickan a potion for bitterness never entered the mouth of mortal man. Oh, I am ruined, poisoned, and undone!'

With that poor Colin drew his plaid over his head, fell flat on his face, and wept bitterly, while his two comely visitants withdrew, smiling at the success of their mission. As they went down by the side of the Feathen-wood, the one said to the other, 'Did you not perceive two of that infatuated community haunting this poor hapless youth to destruction? Let us go and hear their schemes, that we may the better counteract them.'

They skimmed over the lea fields, and, in a thicket

of brambles, briers, and nettles, they found—not two hares, but the identical Rob Kirkwood, the warlock, and auntie Nans, in close and unholy consultation. This bush has often been pointed out to me as the scene of that memorable meeting. It perhaps still remains at the side of a little hollow, nigh to the east corner of the Feathen arable fields, and the spots occupied by the witch and warlock, without a green shrub on them, are still as visible as on the day they left them. The two sisters, having chosen a disguise that completely concealed them, heard the following dialogue, from beginning to end.

'Kimmer, I trow the prize is won. I saw his arm bared; the red blood streaming; the scroll in the one hand, and the pen in the other. He's ours! he's ours!'

'He's nae mair yours.'

'We'll ower the kirkstyle an' away wi' him.'

'I liked not the appearance of yon two pale hinds at such a moment. I wish the fruit of all our pains be not stolen from us when ready for our lord and master's board. How he will storm and misuse us if this has befallen!'

'What of the two hinds? What of them, I say? I like to see blood. It is a beautiful thing blood.'

'Thou art as gross as flesh and blood itself, and hast nothing in thee of the true sublimity of a supernatural being. I love to scale the thundercloud; to ride on the topmost billow of the storm; to roost by the cataract, or croon the anthem of hell at the gate of heaven. But *thou* delightest to see blood,—rank, reeking, and baleful Christian blood. What is in that, dotard?'

'Humph! I like to see Christian blood; howsomever.

It bodes luck, kimmer—it bodes luck.'

'It bodes that thou art a mere block, Rob Kirkwood; but it is needless to upbraid thee, senseless as thou art. List then to me:—It has been our master's charge to us these seven years to gain that goodly stripling, my nephew; and you know that you and I engaged to accomplish it; if we break that engagement, woe unto us. Our master bore a grudge at his father; but he particularly desires the son, because he knows that, could we gain him, all the pretty girls of the parish would flock to our standard.—But, Robin Kirkwood, I say, Robin Kirkwood, what two white birds are these always hopping around us? I dinna like their looks unco weel. See, the one of them is lame too; and they seem to have a language of their own to one another. Let us leave this place, Robin; my heart is quaking like an aspin.'

'Let them hap on. What can wee bits o' birdies do till us? Come, let us try some o' yon cantrips the deil learned us. Grand sport yon, Nans.'

'Robin, did not you see that the birds hopped three times round us? I am afraid we are charmed to the spot.'

'Never mind, auld fool! It's a very good spot.—Some of our cantrips! some of our cantrips!'

What cantrips they performed is not known; but, on that day fortnight, the two were found still sitting in the middle of the bush, the two most miserable and disgusting figures that ever shocked humanity. Their cronies came with a hurdle to take them home; but Nans expired by the way, uttering wild gibberish and blasphemy, and Rob Kirkwood died soon after he got home. The last words he uttered were, 'Plenty o' Christian blood soon! It will be running in streams!—in streams!—in streams!'

We now return to Colin, who, freed of his two greatest adversaries, now spent his time in a state bordering on happiness, compared with the life he had formerly led. He wept much, staid on the hill by himself, and pondered deeply on something nobody knew what, and it was believed he did not know well himself. He was in love—over head and ears in love; which may account for anything in man, however ridiculous. He was in love with Barbara Stewart, an angel in loveliness as well as virtue; but she had hitherto shunned a young man so dissolute and unfortunate in connexions. To this was attributed Colin's melancholy and retirement from society; and it might be partly the case, but there were other matters that troubled his inmost soul.

Ever since he had been visited by the two mysterious dames, he had kept the vial close in his bosom, and had drunk of the bitter potion again and again. He felt a change within him, a certain renovation of his nature, and a new train of thoughts, to which he was an utter stranger; yet he cherished them, tasting oftener and oftener his vial of bitterness, and always, as he drank, the liquor increased in quantity.

While in this half-resigned, half-desponding state, he ventured once more to visit Barbara. He thought to himself that he would go and see her, if but to take farewell of her; for he resolved not to harass so dear a creature with a suit which was displeasing to her. But, to his utter surprise, Barbara received him kindly. His humbled look made a deep impression on her; and, on taking leave, he found that she had treated him with as much respect as any virtuous maiden could treat a favourite lover.

He therefore went home rather too much uplifted in spirit, which his old adversaries, the witches, perceived, and having laid all their snares open to intrap him, they in part prevailed, and he returned, in the moment of temptation, to his old courses. The day after, as he went out to the hill, he whistled and sung,—for he durst not think,—till, behold, at a distance, he saw his two lovely monitors approaching. He was confounded and afraid, for he found his heart was not right for the encounter; so he ran away with all his might, and hid himself in the Feathen-wood.

As soon as he was alone, he took the vial from his bosom, and, wondering, beheld that the bitter liquid was dried up all to a few drops, although the glass was nearly full when he last deposited it in his bosom. He set it eagerly to his lips, lest the last remnant should have escaped him; but never was it so bitter as now; his very heart and spirit failed him, and, trembling, he lay down and wept. He tried again to drain out the dregs of his cup of bitterness; but still, as he drank, it increased in quantity, and became more and more palatable; and he now continued the task so eagerly, that in a few days it was nearly full.

The two lovely strangers coming now often in his mind, he regretted running from them, and wearied once more to see them. So, going out, he sat down within the fairy ring, on the top of the Feathen Hill, with a sort of presentiment that they would appear to him. Accordingly, it was not long till they made their appearance, but still at a distance, as if travelling along the kirk-road. Colin, perceiving that they were going to pass, without looking his way, thought it his duty now to wait on them. He hasted across the moor, and met them; nor did they now shun him. The one that halted now addressed him, while she who had formerly accosted him, and presented him with the vial, looked shy, and kept a marked distance, which Colin was exceedingly sorry for, as he loved her best. The other examined him sharply concerning all his transactions since they had last met. He acknowledged everything candidly—the great folly of which he had been guilty, and likewise the great terror he was in of being changed into some horrible bestial creature, by the bitter drug they had given him. 'For d'ye ken, madam,' said he, 'I fand the change beginning within, at the very core o' the heart, and spreading aye outward and outward, and I lookit aye every minute when my hands and my feet wad change into clutes; for I expeckit nae less than to have another turn o' the gait, or some waur thing, kenning how well I deserved it. And when I saw that I keepit my right proportions, I grat for my ain wickedness, that had before subjected me to such unhallowed influence.'

The two sisters now looked to each other, and a heavenly benevolence shone through the smiles with which that look was accompanied. The lame one said, 'Did I not say, sister, that there was some hope?' She then asked a sight of his vial, which he took from his bosom, and put into her hands; and when she had viewed it carefully, she returned it, without any injunction; but taking from her own bosom a medal of pure gold, which seemed to have been dipped in blood, she fastened it round his neck with a chain of steel. 'As long as you keep that vial and use it,' said she, 'the other will never be taken from you, and with these two you may defy all the Powers of Darkness.'

As soon as Colin was alone, he surveyed his purple meal with great earnestness, but could make nothing of it; there was a mystery in the character and figures of which he had no comprehension; yet he kept all in close concealment, and walked softly.

The witches now found that he was lost to their community, and, enraged beyond measure at the loss of such a prize, which they had judged fairly their own, and of which their master was so desirous, they now laid a plan to destroy him.

He went down to the castle one night to see Barbara Stewart, who talked to him much of religion and of the Bible; but of these things Colin knew very little. He engaged, however, to go with her to the house of prayer—not to the Popish chapel, where he had once been a most irreverent auditor, but to the Reformed church, which then began to divide the parish, and the pastor of which was a devout man.

On taking leave of Barbara, and promising to attend her on the following Sabbath, a burst of eldrich laughter arose close by, and a voice, with a hoarse and giggling sound, exclaimed, 'No sae fast, canny lad—no sae fast. There will maybe be a whipping o' cripples afore that play be played.'

Barbara consigned them both to the care of the

Almighty with great fervency, wondering how they could have been watched and overheard in such a place. Colin trembled from head to foot, for he knew the laugh too well to be that of Maude Stott, the leading witch of the Traquair gang, now that his aunt was removed. He had no sooner crossed the Quair, than, at the junction of a little streamlet, called to this day *the Satyr Sike*, he was set upon by a countless number of cats, which surrounded him, making the most infernal noises, and putting themselves into the most threatening attitudes. For a good while they did not touch him, but leaped around him, often as high as his throat, screaming most furiously; but at length his faith failed him, and he cried out in utter despair. At that moment, they all closed upon him, some round his neck, some round his legs, and some endeavouring to tear out his heart and bowels. At length one or two that came into contact with the medal in his bosom fled away, howling most fearfully, and did not return. Still he was in great jeopardy of being instantly torn to pieces; on which he flung himself flat on his face in the midst of his devouring enemies, and invoked a sacred name. That moment he felt partial relief, as if some one were driving them off one by one, and on raising his head, he beheld his lovely lame visitant of the mountains, driving these infernals off with a white wand, and mocking their threatening looks and vain attempts to return. 'Off with you, poor infatuated wretches!' cried she: 'Minions of perdition, off to your abodes of misery and despair! Where now is your boasted whipping of cripples? See if one poor cripple cannot whip you all.'

By this time the monsters had all taken their flight, save one, that had fastened its talons in Colin's left side, and was making a last and desperate effort to reach his vitals; but he, being now freed from the rest, lent it a blow with such good-will, as made it speedily desist, and fly tumbling and mewing down the brae. He shrewdly guessed who this inveterate assailant was. Nor was he mistaken; for next day Maude Stott was lying powerless on account of a broken back, and several of her cronies were in great torment, having been struck by the white rod of the Lady of the Moor.

But the great Master Fiend, seeing now that his emissaries were all baffled and outdone, was enraged beyond bounds, and set himself, with all his wit, and with all his power, to be revenged on poor Colin. As to his power, no one disputed it; but his wit and ingenuity appear always to me to be very equivocal. He tried to assault Colin's humble dwelling that same night, in sundry terrific shapes; but many of the villagers perceived a slender form, clothed in white, that kept watch at his door until the morning twilight. The next day, he haunted him on the hill in the form of a great shaggy bloodhound, infected with madness; but finding his utter inability to touch him, he uttered a howl that made all the hills quake, and, like a flash of lightning, darted into Glendean's Banks.

He now set himself, with his noted sapience, to procure Colin's punishment by other means, namely, by the hands of Christian men, the only way now left for him. He accordingly engaged his emissaries to inform against him to holy Mother Church, as a warlock and necromancer. The crown and the church had at that time joined in appointing judges of these difficult and interesting questions. The quorum consisted of seven, including the King's Advocate, being an equal number of priests and laymen, all of them in opposition to the principles of the Reformation, it being at that time obnoxious at court. Colin was seized, arraigned, and lodged in prison at Peebles; and never was there such a stir of clamour and discontent in Strath-quair. The young women wept, and tore their hair, for the goodliest lad in the valley; their mothers scolded; and the old men scratched their grey polls, bit the lip, and remained quiescent, but were at length compelled to join the combination.

Colin's trial came on, and his accusers being summoned as witnesses against him, it may well be supposed how little chance he had of escaping, especially as the noted David Beaton sat that day as judge, a severe and bigoted Papist. There were many things proven against poor Colin,—as much as would have brought all the youth of Traquair to the stake; but the stories of the deponents were so monstrous, and so far out of the course of nature, that the judges were like to fall from their seats with laughing.

For instance, three sportsmen swore, that they had started a large he-fox in the Feathen-wood, and, after pursuing him all the way to Glenrath-hope, with horses and hounds, on coming up they found Colin Hyslop lying panting in the midst of the hounds, and caressing and endeavouring to pacify them. It was deponed, that he had been discovered in the shape of a huge gander sitting on eggs; in the shape of a three-legged stool, which had groaned, and given other symptoms of animation, by which its identity with Colin Hyslop was discovered, on being tossed about and overturned, as three-legged stools are apt to be.

But when they came to the story of a he-goat, which had proceeded to attend the service in the chapel of St John the Evangelist, and which said he-goat proved to be the unhappy delinquent, Beaton growled with rage and indignation, and said, that such a dog deserved to suffer death by a thousand tortures, and to be excluded from the power of repentance by the instant infliction of them. The most of the judges were not, however, satisfied of the authenticity of this monstrous story, and insisted on examining a great number of witnesses, both young and old, many of whom happened to be unconnected with the horrid community of the Traquair witches. Among the rest, a girl named Tibby Frater was examined about that, as well as the three-legged stool, and her examination may here be copied verbatim. The querist, who was a cunning man, began as follows:—

'Were you in St John's Chapel, Isabel, on the Sunday after Easter?'

'Yes.'

'And did you there see a man metamorphosed into a he-goat?'

'I saw a gait in the chapel that day.'

'And did he, as has been declared, seem intent on disturbing divine worship?'

'He was playing some pranks. But what else could you expect of a gait?'

'Please to describe what you saw.'

'Oo, he was just rampauging about, an' dinging folk ower. The clerk and the sacristan baith ran to attack him, but he soon held them baith prostrate. Mess John prayed against him, in Latin, they said, and tried to lay him, as if he had been a deil; but he never heedit that, and just rampit on.'

'Did he ever come near or molest you in the chapel?'

'Ay, he did that.'

'What did he do to you?—describe it all.'

'Oo, he didna do that muckle ill, after a'; but if it was the poor young man that was changed, I'll warrant he had nae hand in it, for dearly he paid the kane. Ere long there were fifty staves raised against him, and he was beaten till there was hardly life left in him.'

'And what were the people's reasons for believing that this he-goat and the prisoner were the same?'

'He was found a' wounded and bruised the next day. But, in truth, I believe he never denied these changes wrought on to him to his intimate friends; but we a'ken weel wha it was that effected them. Od help you! ye little ken how we are plaguit and harassed down yonder-abouts, and what loss the country suffers by the emissaries o' Satan! If there be any amang you that ken the true marks o' the beast, you will discern plenty o' them hereabout, some that hae been witnessing against this poor abused and unfortunate young man.'

The members of the community of Satan were now greatly astounded. Their eyes gleamed with vengeance, and they gnashed their teeth on the maiden. But the buzz ran through the assembly against them, and execrations were poured from every corner of the crowded court. Cries of—'Plenty o' proof o' what Tibby has said.'—'Let the saddle be laid on the right horse.'—'Down wi' the plagues o' the land,' and many such exclamations were sent forth from the mouths of the good people of Traquair. They durst not meddle with the witches at home, because, when anything was done to disoblige them, the sheep and the cattle were seized with new and frightful distempers, the corn and barley were shaken, and the honest people themselves quaked under agues, sweatings, and great horrors of mind. But now that they had them all collected in a court of justice, and were all assembled themselves, and holy men present, they hoped to bring the aggressors to due punishment at last. Beaton, however, seemed absolutely bent on the destruction of Colin, alleging, that the depravity of his heart was manifest in every one of his actions during the times of his metamorphoses, even although he had no share himself in effecting these metamorphoses; he therefore sought a verdict against the prisoner, as did also the King's Advocate. Sir James Stewart of Traquair, however, rose up, and spoke with great eloquence and energy in favour of his vassal, and insisted on having his accusers tried face to face with him, when, he had no doubt, it would be seen on which side the sorcery had been exercised. 'For I appeal to your honourable judgments,' continued he, 'if any man would transform himself into a fox, for the sake of being hunted to death, and torn into pieces by hounds? Neither, I think, would any person choose to translate himself into a gander, for the purpose of bringing out a few worthless goslings. But, above all, I am morally certain, that no living woman or man would turn himself into a three-legged stool, for no other purpose but to be kicked into the mire, as the evidence shows this stool to have been. And as for a very handsome youth turning himself into a he-goat, in order to exhibit his prowess in outbraving and beating the men of the whole congregation, that would be a supposition equally absurd. But as we have a thousand instances of honest men being affected and injured by spells and enchantments, I give it as my firm opinion, that this young man has been abused grievously in this manner, and that these his accusers, afraid of exposure through his agency, are trying in this way to put him down.'

Sir James's speech was received with murmurs of applause through the whole crowded court; but the principal judge continued obstinate, and made a speech in reply. Being a man of a most austere temperament, and as bloody-minded as obstinate, he made no objections to the seizing of the youth's accusers, and called to the officers to guard the door; on which the old sacristan of Traquair remarked aloud, 'By my faith in the holy Apostle John, my lord governor, you must be quick in your seizures; for an ye gie but the witches o' Traquair ten minutes, ye will hae naething o' them but moorfowls an' patricks blattering about the rigging o' the kirk; and a' the offishers ye have will neither catch nor keep them.'

They were, however, seized and incarcerated. The trials lasted for three days, at which the most amazing crowds attended; for the evidence was of the most extraordinary nature ever elicited, displaying such a system of diablerie, malevolence, and unheard-of wickedness, as never came to light in a Christian land. Seven women and two men were found guilty, and condemned to be burnt at the stake; and several more would have shared the same fate, had the private marks, which were then thoroughly and perfectly known, coincided with the evidence produced. This not having been the case, they were banished out of the Scottish dominions, any man being at liberty to shoot them, if found there under any shape whatever, after sixty-one hours from that date.

There being wise men who attended the courts in those days, called Searchers or Triers, they were ordered to take Colin into the vestry (the trials having taken place in a church), and examine him strictly for the diabolical marks. They could find none; but in the course of their investigation they found the vial in his bosom, as well as the medal that wore the hue of blood, and which was locked to his neck, so that the hands of man could not remove it. They returned to the judge, bearing the vial in triumph, and saying they had found no private mark, as proof of the master he served, but that here was an unguent, which they had no doubt was proof sufficient, and would, if they judged aright, when accompanied by proper incantations, transform a human into any beast or monster intended. It was handed to the judge, who shook his head, and acquiesced with the searchers. It was then handed around, and Mr Wiseheart, or Wishart, a learned man, deciphered these words on it, in a sacred language,—'The Vial of Repentance.'

The judges looked at one another when they heard these ominous words so unlooked for; and Wiseheart remarked, with a solemn assurance, that neither the term nor the cup of bitterness were calculated for the slaves of Satan, nor the bounden drudges of the land of perdition.

The searchers now begged the Court to suspend their judgment for a space, as the prisoner wore a charm of a bloody hue, which was locked to his body with steel, so that no hands could loose it, and which they judged of far more ominous import than all the proofs of these whole trials put together. Colin was then brought into the Court once more, and the medal examined carefully; and lo! on the one side were engraved, in the same character, two words, the signification of which was decided to be, 'Forgiveness' above, and 'Accceptance' below. On the other side was a representation of the Cruxifixion, and these words in another language, *Cruci, dum spiro, fido;* which words I do not understand, but they struck the judges with great amazement. They forthwith ordered the bounds to be taken off the prisoner, and commanded him to speak for himself, and tell, without fear and dread, how he came by these precious and holy bequests.

Colin, who was noted for sincerity and simplicity, began and related the circumstances of his life, his temptations, his follies, and his disregard of all the duties of religion, which had subjected him in no common degree to the charms and enchantments of his hellish neighbours, whose principal efforts and energies seemed to be aimed at his destruction. But when he came to the vision of the fair virgins on the hill, and of their gracious bequests, that had preserved him thenceforward, both from the devil in person, and from the vengeance of all his emissaries combined, so well did this suit the strenuous efforts then making to obtain popularity for a falling system of faith, that the judges instantly claimed the miracle to their own side, and were clamorous with approbation of his modesty, and cravings of forgiveness for the insults and contumely which they had heaped upon this favourite of Heaven. Barbara Stewart was at this time sitting on the bench close behind Colin, weeping for joy at this favourable turn of affairs, having, for several days previous to that, given up all hopes of his life, when Mr David Beaton pointing to the image of the Holy Virgin, asked if the fair dame who bestowed these invaluable and heavenly relics bore any resemblance to that divine figure. Colin, with his accustomed blunt honesty, was just about to answer in negative, when Barbara exclaimed in a whisper behind him, 'Ah! how like!'

'How do you ken, dearest Barbara?' said he, softly, over his shoulder.

'Because I saw her watching your door once when surrounded by fiends—Ah! how like!'

'Ah, how like!' exclaimed Colin, by way of response to one whose opinion was to him as a thing sacred, and not to be disputed. How much hung on that moment! A denial would would still have subjected hm to obloquy, bonds, and death, but an anxious maiden's ready expedient saved him; and now it was with difficulty that Mr Wiseheart could prevent the Catholic part of the throng from falling down and worshipping him, whom they had so lately reviled and accused of the blackest crimes.

Times were now altered with Colin Hyslop. David Beaton, the governor of the land, appointed by the court of France, took him to Edinburgh in his chariot, and presented him to the Queen Regent, who put a ring on his right hand, a chain of gold about his neck, and loaded him with her bounty. All the Catholic nobles of the court presented him with valuable gifts, and then he was caused to make the tour of all the rich abbeys of Fife and the Border; so that, without ever having one more question asked him about his tenets, he returned home the richest man of all Traquair, even richer, as men supposed, than Sir James Stuart himself. He married Barbara Stewart, and purchased the Plora from the female heirs of Alexander Murray, where he built a mansion, planted a vineyard, and lived in retirement and happiness till the day of his death.

I have thus recorded the leading events of this tale, although many of the incidents, as handed down by tradition, are of so heinous a nature as not to bear recital. It has always appeared to me to have been moulded on the bones of some ancient religious allegory, and by being thus transformed into a nursery tale, rendered unintelligible. It would be in vain now to endeavour to restore its original structure, in the same way as Mr Blore can delineate an ancient abbey from the smallest remnant, but I should like exceedingly to understand properly what was represented by the lovely and mysterious sisters, one of whom was lame. It is most probable that they were supposed apparitions of renowned female saints; or perhaps

Faith and Charity. This, however, is manifest, that it is a Reformer's tale, founded on a Catholic allegory. Of the witches of Traquair there are many traditions extant, as well as many authentic records, and so far the tale accords with the history of the times. That they were tried and suffered there is no doubt; and the Devil lost all his popularity in that district ever after, being despised by his friends for his shallow and rash politics, and hooted and held up to ridicule by his enemies. I still maintain, that there has been no great personage since the world was framed, so apt to commit a manifest blunder, and to overshoot his mark, as he is.

from Blackwood's Edinburgh Magazine
Vol. XXIII (April 1828)

THE WITCHES' CHANT

The women of the Linns invoke supernatural forces to assist them in telling Gelon Graeme of her future. But something is off-key, out of harmony . . .

The Witches' Cot

(*Discovers GRIMALD, NORA, and GELON, standing by a Fire, at which is placed a Waxen Image.*)

GELON. Are these unearthly orgies done?

GRIMALD. Scarce begun!—Scarce begun!—
Come, sing one other strain with me,
To charm the spirit of destiny.

(They sing slowly and wild.)

Where art thou? Where art thou?
  Busy Spirit, where art thou
Weaving the fates of mortals now?
  Where art thou? &c.

GRIMALD. (*Speaks.*) Where art thou? Where art thou?
Busy Spirit, where art thou
Weaving the fates of mortals now?
Art thou beneath the ocean wave,
Scraping the sea-weeds from the grave
Where the merry sailor must shortly lie?
O art thou gone to bustle and ply
Where flaring standards flap the sky,
Working thy baleful web of woe,
Or binding wreaths for the hero's brow?
Or art thou gone to heaven above,
Away to the waning star of love,

To skim the dew-web from the tree,
Of which the golden skene shall be
That guides the lover's destiny?
Or watchest thou the stripling's bed,
Or the couch where maiden beauty is laid,
With dreams their feelings to suborn,
And sprinkle from thy living urn
The kindred spark that long shall burn?
Spirit! wherever thou may'st be,
Or gone to the caves beneath the sea,
Or flown the wild sea-rock to haunt
And scare the drowsy cormorant;
Whether thou rangest vale or steep,
Or watchest mellow beauty's sleep,
The monarch's throne, or the field of death,
The world above, or the world beneath,
We ask thy welcome presence here,
Come—Come—Appear—Appear.

(Pause)

I see thee not—I cannot see
The slighest shade or drapery
Of fate's own herald, known to me.
O come like a feeling, or come like a sound,
Or come like an odour along the ground;
Come like a film of floating blue,
Or come like the moss-crop's slightest flue,
Or glimmering rack of the midnight dew.
We wait thee motionless and dumb—
Come, O gentle Spirit! come.

(Pause.)

Oh me! there is trouble and torsel here;
Some countervailing spirit is near,

Who will not let the gye appear.
Sister, go to the door and see;
Note the sound that comes from the tree,
And the vapour that sleeps on the midnight lea.
Note if the shred of silver grey
Floats o'er the belt of the starry ray,
Or streams in the cleft of the milky-way.
And look between the north and the east
For the star above the mountain's crest
That changes still its witching hue,—
Note if it's green, or red, or blue.

(Exit NORA.)

This is a night of mystery!
Maiden, say a hymn with me.

(They sing soft and slow.)

Thou art weary, weary, weary!
  Thou art weary and far away!
Hear me, gentle Spirit, hear me!
  Come before the dawn of day!
    Thou art weary, &c.

(Re-enter NORA.)

Say, bodes the night's eye well or ill?
NORA. I heard a small voice from the hill;
The vapour is deadly, pale, and still.
A murmuring sough is on the wood,
And the little star is red as blood.
Moules sits not on his throne to-night,
For there is not a hue of the grizly light;
But in the cleft of heaven I scan
The giant form of a naked man;
His eye is like the burning brand,
And he holds a sword in his right hand.

GRIMALD. All is not well!

　By dint of spell,

Somewhere between the heavens and hell,

There is this night a wild deray,

The spirits have wandered from their way!

And the purple drops shall tinge the moon

As she wanders through the midnight noon;

And the dawning heaven shall all be red

With aerial blood by angels shed.

　Be as it will,

　I have the skill

To work by good, or to work by ill.

(They prick the Image alternately with sharp
bodkins.)

Take that for pain!

NORA. And that for thrall!

GRIMALD. And that for conscience, the worst of all!

If spirits come not, mortals shall!

Another chaunt, and then, and then,

From the but or from the ben,

Spirits shall come or christian men.

(They chant.)

　Where is Gil-Moules,

　Where is Gil-Moules,

Works he not save when the tempest howls?

　Where is Gil-Moules, &c.

GRIMALD. (Speaks.) Sleep'st thou, wakest thou, lord
　of the wind?

Mount thy steeds and gallop them blind,

Leave the red thunder-bolt lagging behind;

And the long-tail'd fiery dragon outfly,

The rocket of heaven, the bomb of the sky;

Over the dog-star, over the wain,
Over the cloud and the rainbow's mane;
Over the mountain and over the sea,
Haste, haste, haste to me!
            (They pierce the Figure alternately.)
Take that for trouble!
NORA. And that for smart!
GRIMALD. And that for the pang that seeks the heart!
NORA. That for madness!
GRIMALD. And that for thrall!
And that for conscience, the worst of all!

from All-Hallow-Eve